The Audiovisual Teacher

Written by
Julian Costa

Library of Congress Cataloging-in-Publication Data:

Names:	Costa, Julian Thomas, 1989–, author
Title:	The Audiovisual Teacher
ISBN-13:	978-1-957863-27-6
BISAC:	BIO019000 BIOGRAPHY & AUTOBIOGRAPHY / Educators
	EDU029000 EDUCATION / Teaching Methods & Materials / General

Copyeditor/Proofreader:	Angel Ackerman
Layout Design:	Julian Costa
Design Assistance:	Gary Snyder
Printer and Binder:	Ingram Sparks

Photography credits: Gary Braman, Charles Kagel, Michael Weaver
Additional photo sources listed in the reference section.
All photos are used for editorial purposes only.
Cover photo: dihandrea/pexels.com (edited)

CONNECT with the publisher:

Substack:	parisianphoenixpublishing.substack.com
Web:	www.ParisianPhoenix.com
Facebook:	@parisianphoenixpublishing
Instagram:	@parisianphoenix
LinkedIn:	@parisianphoenixpublishing
Patreon:	@parisianphoenix
TikTok:	@parisianphoenix

parisian phoenix
PUBLISHING

Published by Parisian Phoenix Publishing, Easton, Pennsylvania USA
Printed in the United States of America.

Table of Contents

Dedication

This book is dedicated to the memory of

Hamilton Hang Tao Lee
October 10, 1921 – March 14, 2018

Preface

Picture a twentieth-century classroom — what do you see? Students seated in desks, facing the lecturer at the front of the room. Other than writing on the chalkboard, there is very little variety in terms of instructional delivery.

If you think it seems ineffective, even stale, you are not alone. Many educators were aware of the faults of education and sought more engaging ways of facilitating learning. This charming little book tells the story of one of those educators.

Dr. Hamilton Hang Tao Lee, born in China, followed his intrigue regarding educational systems to study pedagogy and its associated technology internationally. In the mid-1950s, he left his home country in pursuit of graduate study in education at a time when audio-visual technology was pouring into schools across the globe.

Though Lee's curricular emphasis was instructional technology, he was much more than a lover of technology. The story of Dr. Lee's career, which spanned from the 1940s to the 1980s, encompasses intercultural communication, a rich appreciation for the humanities, and a fascination with teaching and learning in its purest sense. He began his journey as a high school teacher in Taiwan, teaching Chinese and English language courses at rural schools. Upon immigrating to the United States, he earned two graduate degrees, both in

1

education, in quick succession. During this time, he discovered his specialty: audio-visual education. As a university professor, Lee developed and taught courses in this area for nearly twenty years. While Lee's teaching focus was to help teacher education majors develop technical competencies, his interest in the teaching of language and the humanities was much more satisfying to him. Later in life, Lee found his creative outlet through writing poetry.

As an undergraduate student who had recently transferred to a new university, I was curious to learn about the school's history and, in particular, how the teaching of technology had evolved over the years. On a cold winter day, I browsed the university catalog collection in East Stroudsburg University's library where I stumbled across the name, "Hamilton Lee." I saw his name appear in numerous volumes, but found very little else. Over the next two years, only four photographs of Lee materialized.

As it turned out, to the chagrin of this writer, very few records of Lee's accomplishments survive today. It was not long before I felt determined to learn more about this man. Since his career was prior to the advent of the Internet, most of the research for this book required exhaustive searches through paper records and print media. Records maintained at Lee's long-time place of work, East Stroudsburg University of Pennsylvania, allowed me to assemble a timeline of Lee's career and learn about his tangible accomplishments.

A poetry anthology he wrote in retirement provided some clues into Lee's emotions at various stages of his life. Due to the scarcity of information available, this book will take three forms: a historical overview of the educational system in China during Lee's formative years; a biography of Lee's career; and a summary of Lee's poetic works. It is my hope that biography and life writing will someday be recognized as a more respectable form of scholarship, in that it can provide inspiration to our next generation of educators while keeping readers connected to our disciplinary roots.

For clarification, I provide these notes for the reader: Dr. Lee's name at birth was Hang Tao Lee, which was legally changed to Hamilton H.T. Lee in 1966. Lee will be referenced in the book by his legal name at that point in his life. East Stroudsburg State College was renamed East Stroudsburg University in 1983, thus, the institutional title of the year in reference will be utilized. Consistent with the style of Lee's day, the term "audio-visual" is hyphenated, unless the source text did not include a hyphen.

Certainly, there is much more to learn about Hamilton Lee, but I feel confident that this book will help to start the conversation. This book will hopefully motivate other educators and technologists to celebrate the people who contributed to the study of instructional technology. As technology evolves, it is very easy to forget what came before it. I hope that our knowledge of this evolution, and those whose careers spanned that evolution, do not drift into oblivion as quickly as we might throw a typewriter or a VCR into the garbage.

A student delivering a videotaped "microteaching" lesson,
East Stroudsburg State College, 1973.

Acknowledgements

For as much of a solitary, monkish activity as writing can be, no project of this scale can be completed alone. A heartfelt thank you is extended to Angel R. Ackerman at Parisian Phoenix Publishing for believing in this project, and to Nicolas Kratzel for providing research assistance.

In the spirit of education, I am grateful to the faculty at my alma mater, East Stroudsburg University, for embracing my fascination with archival research. Dr. Elzar Camper, Jr., Professor Emeritus, was kind enough to take many strolls down memory lane with me. It was wonderful to get reacquainted with you after nearly a decade. Dr. Richard Otto, Associate Professor of Media and my undergraduate advisor, always saw the value of my work long before I did and made excellent recommendations.

Many individuals made the early stages of this research possible through their contributions and votes of support as far back as my undergraduate years Douglas Smith, Brenda Friday, and Sheree Watson of the Office of University Relations, East Stroudsburg University; Nancy Boyer and Laurie Schaller of the East Stroudsburg University Foundation; and Professors Leslie Berger and Patricia Jersey of Kemp Library. Thank you all for providing that young researcher (me) with access to archival materials and for sharing your recollections of days gone by.

This project was also made possible through the wonderful contributions of passionate and caring educators across the country who share a love of history and a desire to preserve it properly. Dr. Alan Delozier, Seton Hall University Archives; Erin Spierings and Ilariah McAnally, University of Wisconsin at La Crosse; Angela Beaton, Minnesota State University; Rebecca Toov, University of Minnesota; and Elizabeth Clemens, Wayne State University, have accommodated my many requests for information and were always efficient and prompt…even during a pandemic. Dr. Ruth Hayhoe of the University of Toronto shared valuable resources. Of all of the great individuals who have helped me track down information for this book, I am most indebted to Sarah Lebovitz of Wayne State University's library. Her helpful recommendations and sincere excitement toward this project are deeply appreciated.

To Gayle F. Hendricks, design professor at Northampton Community College, thank you for your continued guidance and tutoring on the design process. To my dearly departed mentor and friend, Dr. Rebecca Dean, your contributions to education will forever be an inspiration.

Much recognition is owed to my colleagues at Pace University, specifically Dr. Joseph Lee (no relation to Hamilton Lee) and Brian Moses, for tracking down resources I needed and making excellent recommendations on the direction of the research. To my departmental colleagues and beloved friends, Mary Stambaugh and Barry Morris, your enthusiasm and faith in my abilities have impacted me more than you know.

Finally, I would be remiss if I did not thank the young people in my life: my niece, Rosalie Michalak, and my godchildren, David and Aliyah Montes, whose names I so enjoy seeing in print. May you always enjoy learning, may you appreciate the story in all things, big and small, and always know how much you are loved.

Julian Costa
May 2024

Beginnings

On October 10, 1921, in the Chinese province of Shantung, Beiyuen and Huaiying Lee welcomed their son, Hang Tao, into the world. While little is known about Lee's parents or his upbringing, his later writings imply a warm, loving relationship with his parents, particularly with his mother. At some point during his childhood, Lee and his family left Shantung (today's Shandong) and moved to Formosa, Taiwan, a mountainous island that was described by Portuguese sailors as *ilha formosa*, or "beautiful island." From a young age, Lee was exposed to the arts and found a lot of pleasure in reading literary classics and attending theatrical performances. Of particular interest to Lee was opera, which was a topic that Lee would continue to learn about throughout his life. We can applaud Lee's parents for fostering their son's love for the arts, as it is quite possible that these interests prompted Lee to pursue a Bachelor of Arts degree.

"Incidentally," Lee recalled, "the National Peiping Teachers University from which I was graduated was one of the three most prestigious institutions of higher learning in Peiping, China (perhaps in China)." Upon completing high school in Formosa, Lee relocated to Beijing in 1948 and began his baccalaureate coursework.

The timing of Lee's decision to pursue a career in teaching was interesting. During Lee's upbringing and college years, the Chinese educational system was undergoing major restructuring. As far back as the turn of the century, China was looking to modernize their educational system, largely modeling after the United States' model.

According to a 1979 report written by the National Committee on United States-China Relations, *China's Schools in Flux*, Chinese education during the Kuomintang regime relied heavily on American and European guidance. "The primary and secondary schools located outside of [vicinities of higher education institutions] were concentrated in the provincial capitals and market towns, and many were run with the benefit of foreign assistance derived mainly from missionary sources" (1979, p. 4). The Chinese Communist Party (CCP) soon realized that they needed to develop their own educational system, free of American or European input, that would contribute to the economic development and growth of the nation.

Their guiding principles, which are commendable even by today's standards, focused on reforming the higher education system as well as through developing "…a sufficient number of literate, skilled, and secularized graduates while at the same time providing expansion in all sectors of the economy so that they could be absorbed in ways that were useful to the nation and meaningful to the graduates themselves" (p. 7). Perhaps Lee's educational journey was a product of this philosophy. It is also possible that Lee's decision to pursue a career in teaching was a product of the times. A 1950 report by British educational scholar Michael Lindsay reported that the Northeastern United Executive Committee asserted in 1946 that teacher training in China, particularly of the upper-grades, was considered a first priority (1977, pp. 63-64). It is unclear as to whether or not Lee's decision to pursue a degree in education was the result of political influence.

In 1948, he graduated with a dual Bachelor of Arts degree, majoring in both general studies and education. His diploma, however, was not the only milestone Lee reached during his college years. While studying at Peiping, Lee met Chin Chang, a medical doctor at the Central University of China. They fell in love and were married on August 24, 1945. Lee would spend the rest of his life with her.

Lee began his teaching career at Yuanli High School, located in Hsinchu, Taiwan, where he was assigned to teach English and

Chinese. Originating as an agricultural college during the Japanese colonial period, this school became Miaoli County's junior high school during the 1930s. After one year on the faculty, Lee left for a similar position at Kangshan High School, also located in Taiwan. The second year of his teaching career was a new beginning for two reasons. Aside from being a new place of employment, the beginning of Lee's tenure coincided with the proclamation of the People's Republic of China, a pivotal point in Chinese history and the beginning of communist rule.

In 1988, sociologist and Hong Kong native Julia Kwong, described the communist government taking an active role in the oversight of the education system in her book, *Cultural Revolution in China's Schools*:

> Missionary and private schools came under direct official super vision, and the government expanded the provisions for secondary education more than eleven times and of primary education five times between 1949 and 1965. More important, new curricula were drafted for the nation's primary and secondary schools to conform to the hegemonic ideology of communism (1988, p. xiii).

Many agreed at the time that an overhaul of China's educational history was necessary, but many educators who had embraced a Confucian approach to teaching, did not happily accept the Marxist philosophy being instituted by the communist party.

Lee, having completed his education prior to the communist takeover, had a different outlook on education. It is plausible that he felt pressure from his school's administration to conform his teaching to the directives coming from the government. As Kwong describes, "Since the socialization of the young rested as much on the written curriculum as on the organization of activities in the classroom, an important part of the socialization responsibility rested with the teachers. Teachers ignored, where possible, central regulations incompatible with their own outlook or followed them formally and mechanically if the situation required them to comply" (1988, p. iii). Surely, not all teachers were happy about these regulations, as many educators missed the autonomy that they once had.

During his seven years at Kangshan, Lee continued to teach English. He also began teaching history, and all the while, was likely becoming very uncomfortable with the Taiwanese educational model and considering his own professional growth. He was the recipient of a Teachers' Advancement Fellowship which afforded him the opportunity to pursue development opportunities, however, the lure of a Master's degree made him realize that he would need to relocate.

Since the Chinese educational system as Lee knew it was highly influenced by American educators, it is quite possible that Lee favored their input and was inspired to pursue his graduate study in the United States. Further, it would afford him and his growing family with many opportunities that simply were not available to them in Taiwan. In 1956, Lee made the heartbreaking decision, the pain of which would be evident in the poetry he wrote later in life, to leave China and move to Minneapolis, Minnesota, never to see his parents or childhood home again.

Graduate Studies

A popular adage that pertains to nearly every profession is "you have to go where the jobs are." This applies to the pursuit of education, too. With eight years of teaching experience under his belt, Hang Tao Lee wanted to pursue a graduate degree. With three children in tow, Lee and his wife moved to Minneapolis, Minnesota, where Lee began his graduate coursework at the University of Minnesota.

The University of Minnesota's College of Education offered a comprehensive program for teacher education, professional development, and research. Specialized laboratories, including a model school for teacher training, provided a blend of conceptual instruction and practical application. At the graduate level, one could major in ten different areas of emphasis, which included educational administration. This program was designed for individuals who had completed a Baccalaureate degree in education and had aspirations of earning a school principal or superintendent certification. Students could also elect a minor in another area of education, and were given the option to take additional coursework in place of writing a thesis.

Wesbrook Hall at the University of Minnesota. Audio-Visual Education courses took place on the second floor of this building. It was later demolished in 2011.

Lee elected not to write a thesis, so instead, he declared a minor in Curriculum and Instruction which allowed him to take additional courses of a practical nature. In his third semester at UMN, Lee enrolled in what would be the most influential course he would take: Audio-Visual Materials in Education.

This course, then listed in the university catalog as "Ed.C.I. 105," provided an introduction to audio-visual education, stressed the advantages and limitations of different media as well as how to utilize equipment that was available to teachers. The course was taught by Neville Pearson, who taught all of the Audio-visual Education courses and managed the College's Audio-visual Laboratory.

Pearson, who was a graduate of the University of Minnesota, had begun his career as a teacher at both the junior high and high school levels. He then served as a filmmaker with the Airforce Combat Camera Unit during World War II and made films for the U.S. State Department. By 1957, Pearson was very active on the UMN campus, within the Minneapolis community, and in several state-wide and na-tionwide professional organizations. Furthermore, Pearson relished in research activities and worked with many graduate students on their doctoral dissertations. Whether Lee realized it or not, Pearson was an excellent role model and his career would follow a very similar trajectory.

Lee found his niche and was inspired to continue his studies in this area. Oddly, he did not take any more audio-visual courses at UMN. Regardless, Lee continued to thrive in his studies and in 1957 was awarded the *Foreign Student Tuition Scholarship*. This honor, sponsored by the University's Board of Regents, is "awarded to students from other countries on the basis of outstanding scholarship and promise." Lee graduated with the Master of Arts degree in Educational Administration on August 21, 1958.

Professor Neville Pearson. The camel's name is unknown.

He was one of fifteen students to graduate from this program.

The year 1958 came with another accomplishment in the field of education, though a bit grander than Lee's completion of a graduate degree. To the chagrin of the United States, the Soviet Union launched *Sputnik 1*, the first artificial satellite, into orbit. Losing the "space race" prompted then-president Dwight D. Eisenhower to launch an initiative that would enhance the quality of education in the United States.

Out of this initiative was born *The National Defense Education Act* (NDEA). The act, which was signed into law on September 2, 1958, was broken into ten "titles," or sections that spanned curriculum, funding, and other issues pertinent to a successful educational program. Of particular interest to Lee would be Title VI, which focused on funding for language study, and Title VII, which provided for funding to support educational technology. With both of Lee's professional interests being taken into account under this new act, the pursuit of a doctoral degree became all the more attainable. So, Lee and his family left Minnesota and moved to Detroit, Michigan, where Lee began his doctoral studies only three months after completing his master's degree.

Wayne State University, located in Detroit, offered a Doctor of Education program for educators in a variety of fields. The program offered fifteen different fields of concentration, each requiring eighteen hours of coursework. In addition to one's concentration and the professional theory courses, students in the program were required to enroll in fifteen hours of non-education "cognate" courses, and successfully defend a dissertation. Among the options for concentration was Audio-Visual Education. As one would expect, Lee declared this as his concentration. Since Lee had also taught language courses in the past, it is presumable that his background motivated him to declare minors in linguistics and psychology.

Certainly, to Lee's delight, Wayne State University's College of Education had its own Department of Audio-Visual Education. The department offered eight different graduate courses in audio-visual education, spanning from hands-on training with equipment and materials to administrative considerations. What made the quality of this curriculum even greater was the facilities in which students were taught, as described in the course catalog:

> The Department of Audio-Visual Education provides a laboratory where facilities and materials for making different kinds of instructional materials are available to students. Laboratory staff members assist students in preparing such teaching materials as bulletin board displays, feltboard sets, posters, charts, tape recordings, pictorial exhibits, and slides. The laboratory provides work space for students as well as needed material and equipment, such as lettering devices, air brushes, and slide-making materials. Students may also learn how to operate various types of projectors, recorders, and playbacks (1956, p. 15)

The faculty in the Audio-Visual Education department came from varied backgrounds, including radio station management, educational television, and museum curation. Interestingly, the majority of the faculty only had master's degrees.

Images of students in Wayne State University's Audio-Visual Laboratory, 1950s.

One of Lee's first instructors was Robert Kilbourn, who later became the chairman of the department. Kilbourn, who was pursuing his doctorate at Ohio State University, specialized in audio-visual education and taught several different courses in this area. Another mentor of Lee's was Mr. Thomas Roberts, who served as the Director of the Audio-Visual Center. Roberts, like Lee, was pursuing a terminal degree in instructional technology and was particularly interested in the development of foreign language laboratories. Lee having come to the United States with several years of experience in the teaching of language, such an intellectual commonality was certainly desirable.

Like many graduate students, Lee pursued on-campus employment during his graduate coursework. Fortunately, Wayne State University's Center for Instructional Technology offered him opportunities to develop his technical competencies while learning about the managerial aspects of running an on-campus media production facility.

From as far back as the early 1940s, the University offered media services through the College of Education's Audio-Visual Consultation Bureau. A film library and television studio are two examples of their services. While archival records of this facility are scarce, it is conceivable that the Bureau was the predecessor to the Center for Instructional Technology. Regardless, Lee worked for the Center as a Research Associate from 1956 to 1964. Presumably, Roberts served as Lee's direct supervisor in this role, though documentation of this claim could not be found.

The Center for Instructional Technology at Wayne State University, 1950s.

As an educator and researcher, Lee recognized the importance of becoming involved in the discipline of media. This involvement would provide not only an opportunity to network with like-minded scholars, but also give him access to cutting-edge research on the benefit of audio-visual technology in teaching. Lee quickly became involved in the National Education Association's Department of Audio-Visual Instruction (NEA-DAVI). As a result of his active participation, Lee was awarded two consecutive fellowships from the Learning Resources Corporation based in East Lansing, Michigan.

These fellowships allowed Lee to participate in seminars that, ultimately, acquainted him with the topic he would eventually select for his dissertation: programmed learning. "Programmed materials," as defined by Lee, "are sequentially organized materials written in a highly logical manner from the simple to the complex within a body of knowledge" (1964, p. 17). The "teaching machine," as it was commonly referred to in psychological research, had gained scholarly attention as far back as the 1920s. The programmed learning process can be compartmentalized into three phases: reinforcement, incremental presentation of content, and self-paced learning. A teaching approach such as programmed learning lends itself well to skill attainment, which is especially useful and important in the study of a language. Attainment is the key to successful language learning.

Lee's years at Wayne State were quickly passing. As he decided upon his dissertation research, several circumstances in Taiwan and their impact on the education there influenced Lee. An area that was particularly striking to Lee was the scarcity of language instruction. Though his academic focus had shifted toward instructional technology, Lee was still interested in the teaching of language in secondary education. Moreover, the quality of education in Taiwan continued to pique Lee's interest, especially since compulsory education was limited to six years; there was a shortage of teachers, a growing population, and a changing curriculum.

In the early 1960s, the use of instructional television programs was gaining popularity as an effective solution for large class sizes and limited campus resources at many Taiwanese schools. This, in conjunction with a programmed text, would be an effective solution to the barriers being encountered in Taiwanese high schools. "The [programmed learning] program was designed," Lee explained, "basically for non-English speaking learners, but it also may be used for English speaking students who seek a comprehensive understanding of English structure through a structural linguistic approach" (1964, p. 2). The following passage from Lee's dissertation most succinctly explains his research problem:

The principal purpose of this study is to develop appropriate means to be used in solving two problems: (1) to educate a larger number of pupils; and (2) to accelerate the education processes of school children in Taiwan. Two methods seem promising as solutions to the two problems previously cited: (1) individual self-learning materials, and (2) instructional television programs. Therefore, in this research a model self-instructional program will be developed, and the application of programmed learning materials accompanied by supplementary instructional television programs will also be explored (1964, p. 14)

The success of a dissertation often relies on the qualifications of one's committee. In the case of Lee's dissertation, such a multi-faceted study would require a variety of expertise. Obviously, a faculty member whose scholarly focus is programmed learning would be paramount. Enter: Joseph Hill. Hill, who was the Assistant Dean of the College of Education, was a well-renowned specialist in statistics and research design. He was the founder of the American Association of Educational Sciences, had served as a research design consultant to school districts across the country, and, most relevantly, he was an active member of the Detroit Society for Programmed Instruction. Perhaps what motivated Lee to request Hill's advisership was his having designed an educational program, titled "Personal Educational Programs Using Cognitive Style Mapping," which utilized a self-paced multimedia approach toward learning. This system was used by colleges in both the United States and Canada.

Dr. Joseph Hill

Once Hill was in place on the committee, Lee realized that he needed someone who was an expert in audio-visual education. Thus, he selected his professor, Robert Kilbourn. Kilbourn and Hill served as co-chairs of the dissertation. Since Lee's study focused on secondary education, he asked Theodore Rice to serve as well. With several years of experience as a high school teacher and principal, a school board consultant, and service as the initiator of Oklahoma's *Commission on Teacher Education*, Rice would provide valuable insight into the tenets of contemporary education in the United States. The final member of the committee needed to be someone who was versed in learning behavior. Edward Adamek, who was a professor of theoretics and behavioral foundations, came to the committee having conducted research in the area of "progressive education." The dream team was assembled and work could begin.

To conduct a project of the magnitude of a dissertation, particularly one of a cross-disciplinary focus like this one, a researcher must turn to experts in other fields for consultation. Lee realized that in order to examine the teaching of a language, he would need to fully understand the mechanics of the English language. So, he got in contact with Dr. Donald Lloyd, a Yale University graduate and associate professor of English at Wayne State. A proponent of professional development in the teaching of English, Lloyd conducted workshops and presented research in linguistics, the structure of the English language, and the teaching of English using audio-visual technology. Among his list of publications are several entries in Audio-Visual Instruction and reports on the development of audio-visual language courses. Lloyd's contributions enabled Lee to develop a fifty-three-page programmed textbook that served as a critical component to the dissertation. The text provided instruction in the use of nouns and adjectives. The study never made use of instructional television. Though he did not officially serve on Lee's committee, Lloyd's contributions to the study were immeasurable, as recognized by Lee in the acknowledgements section of the dissertation:

> In developing the programmed text on English structure as a part of the dissertation, Dr. Donald Lloyd, Associate Professor of English, gave his special counsel to the writer. Particularly, without his…permission to use their methods of symbolizing the patterns of statement of English, the writer could not have developed the programmed text (1964, p. iii).

In 1964, alongside nineteen other doctoral candidates, Lee graduated with the Ed.D. degree in Instructional Technology, with minors in linguistics and psychology. While Lee's degree was largely focused on technology, his curiosity into the social sciences persisted. This resulted in his enrolling as a post-doctoral scholar at Wayne State for an additional semester where he studied the psychology of programmed learning and communication.

By this point, Lee had lived in the United States for eight years. In that time, Lee completed two degrees, engaged in scholarly endeavors, developed technical competencies, and was on track to begin his career in higher education. Perhaps less tangibly, Lee's sensitivity to culture and language was paying off in dividends by informing his research and providing him with a context in which to apply his practical knowledge of instructional technology. Lee would never teach a course in language again, however, it would remain a prominent interest of his for the rest of his career.

Design and Development of Programmed Materials for
Secondary English Teaching in Taiwan with Implications
For Future Technological Development in Instructional Procedures

by

Hang Tao Lee

A Dissertation

Submitted to the Graduate Division
of Wayne State University, Detroit, Michigan
in partial fulfillment of the requirements
for the degree of

Doctor of Education

1964

MAJOR: EDUCATION
(INSTRUCTIONAL TECHNOLOGY)

APPROVED BY:

Advisers   Date

The title page of Lee's doctoral dissertation.

Ascending the Ivory Tower

Success in any profession requires belief. Belief in oneself; belief in one's profession. It was with much belief in both of these areas that Hang Tao Lee left Wayne State University and pursued a short but meaningful opportunity.

Just twenty miles west of New York City sat Seton Hall University, a Roman Catholic university that offered a vast selection of programs for undergraduate and graduate study. Seton Hall also offered professional development programs for teachers. Among these programs was The Summer Language Institute, a seven-week intensive program for teachers of Chinese. This program, developed in 1958 under the provisions of *The National Defense Education Act*, worked with elementary and secondary-level teacher teachers to provide them with cultural and linguistic knowledge to enhance their teaching of the Chinese language. Among the objectives of the Institute, one in particular deserves highlighting:

> To improve the teaching effectiveness of the participants by providing training in new teaching methods, the use of new instructional materials and the practical applications of linguistics to the teaching situation (1962).

Lee, being of Chinese origin, having taught the Chinese language to native high school students, and later studying education and instructional technology, such an objective speaks to Lee's areas of contribution. It is not surprising that he would be interested in participating in this program.

Photos from a 1960s brochure for the Summer Language Institute at Seton Hall University. (L) Educators work in the Language Laboratory; (R) an evening conversation under the trees. Dr. John B. Tsu oversees both activities.

In July, 1964, Lee traveled to South Orange, New Jersey to begin his visiting professorship at Seton Hall. According to the limited information available from Lee's curriculum vitae, he taught courses in Chinese Literature for the Summer Language Institute and directed the University's Language Laboratory. The twenty-three-seat laboratory, which had recently been upgraded with media production capabilities, included recording rooms, duplicating machines, and a tape library for independent study.

Certainly, to Lee's delight, Seton Hall was making notable progress in the development of instructional media toward the teaching of language. Dr. John DeFrancis, a research professor of Asian Studies, was heavily involved in the production of media for Chinese language learning. Throughout the 1960s, he published several textbooks and oversaw the recording of multiple accompanying audio programs.

The participants of the Institute were trained in media production, too. At the end of the program, the students prepared a "student show" that was audio recorded for educational and entertainment purposes. While the extent to which Lee was involved is unclear, training teachers on the use of technology to produce media would have been a good fit for him.

After a productive summer of training language teachers at Seton Hall, Lee returned to the Midwest to begin his first tenure-track position at Moorhead State University in Minnesota. Audio-visual education was a prominent aspect of the undergraduate teacher education curriculum. Students at Moorhead also had the option to declare a minor in audio-visual education that included coursework in photography and the preparation of inexpensive instructional materials. In addition to this, certification programs for in-service teachers looking to become audio-visual education coordinators and directors were offered, as well as two graduate courses: "Utilization of Audio-Visual Materials," and "Problems in Audio-Visual Education." The former offered practical training in equipment operation and creation of materials, while the latter allowed the student to pursue an individual research problem. All of this instruction took place in the Livingston Lord Library, which described its then-new facility in the 1964 college catalog:

> The Audio-Visual Center, on the main floor, provides classrooms for Audio-Visual courses and facilities for booking, previewing, producing, and servicing films, film strips, and other audio-visual instructional materials. The center maintains a film library, and prepares various kinds of materials and presentations for instructional use. Consultation services and assistance are provided for on-campus students and faculty, as well as teachers and administrators of the public schools in the area (1964, p. 23).

As an assistant professor of audio-visual education, Lee's primary responsibility was teaching courses in the Center, such as "Audio Visual Methods in Instruction," as well as graduate courses in the utilization of audio-visual materials and research problems in the field.

Advising students in the teacher education program was also an important component of Lee's position. Working alongside colleague Peter Dart, who was a graduate of the University of Indiana, Lee and

Dart served as the faculty advisors for students in the audio-visual education programs as well as for elementary education majors. Lee was selected to serve on the Council of Admissions as well as the Records and Research Committee, which may have been an appointed position.

Concurrently, working in the Audio-Visual Center allowed Lee to conduct in-service workshops for teachers. While Lee's faculty obligations consumed much of his time and energy, he still managed to make time to speak off campus at schools and churches in Minnesota, according to copies of his curriculum vitae. From an outsider's point of view, Lee's position at Moorhead was a perfect fit, allowing him to teach courses in audio-visual education, provide service to teachers, and lend his expertise to the production of media.

Professor Peter Dart

After only one year on the faculty, Lee resigned from his position at Moorhead. Despite a thorough search through the University's archives, no accounts could be located to verify the reasoning behind this move. One can only speculate as to whether Lee was happy or not, whether or not he and his colleagues worked cohesively together, or if administration was pleased with his performance.

Fortunately, Lee had new opportunities awaiting him. In the summer of 1965, Lee left Minnesota and traveled to Harvard University, where he was awarded a postdoctoral scholar appointment to study in the Department of Social Relations. There is no evidence that the summer appointment caused him to leave his position at Moorhead, but perhaps the excitement of studying at an Ivy League school was too great to pass up.

At the intersection of psychology, anthropology, and philosophy, this interdisciplinary program thrived on informal, discussion based courses that examined topics pertaining to culture, comparative politics, and psycholinguistics, among others. Despite the highly technical nature of Lee's field, he clearly had a fascination with the liberal arts, specifically language and cognition, and eagerly engaged in opportunities to learn more about these areas. He spent two consecutive summers at Harvard.

Meanwhile, nearly four hundred miles east of Moorhead sat the town of La Crosse, Wisconsin. The University of Wisconsin-La Crosse began as a normal school (or, a school for training teachers) in the early twentieth century, and even after becoming part of the Wisconsin university system in 1964, continued to invest a lot into teacher preparation programs. Similar to Moorhead, La Crosse housed an audio-visual center within their library that was capable of media production as well as equipment repair. A large library of films and tapes maintained by the center were used across campus.

The Audio-Visual Department at the University of Wisconsin-La Crosse. Clockwise: Florence Wing Technology Center Exterior; the AV Lab; students preparing films for campus distribution; the AV classroom. Image courtesy of Murphy Library Special Collections/ARC, University of Wisconsin-La Crosse.

The University offered several undergraduate courses in audio-visual education, comprising a "service minor" that teaching majors were eligible to declare atop their education course requirements. It could not be determined whether or not education majors at La Crosse were required to complete an audio-visual education course, however, the ED 317 course, titled "Audiovisual Education," was offered each semester throughout the year. In the mid-1960s, audio-visual education courses at La Crosse were taught by Viggio B. Rasmusen, a graduate of the University of Wisconsin-Madison and director of La Crosse's Audiovisual Center, and George Lester Steinhoff, who was an alumnus of Iowa State University. Both of these individuals began their teaching careers as secondary education teachers and served the university through classroom teaching and administering audio-visual services.

Clearly there was a need for growth, as in August of 1965, it was announced that a new faculty position was created for an instructor of audio-visual education. An article in the La Crosse Sunday Tribune announced the hiring of fifty-nine new faculty members, and among them was Hang Tao Lee.

Interestingly, Lee was appointed to the La Crosse faculty at the rank of associate professor. One might question the motivation behind this increase in rank after only one year at the assistant professor level. Perhaps Lee's years of service as a research associate at Wayne State University were taken into consideration.

Similar to his year at Moorhead, Lee was tasked with teaching undergraduate courses for teacher education majors. Specifically, Lee's course load included two sections of AV 203, Production of Audio-Visual Materials, and two sections of the Graphics Lab component of AV 317, Audio-Visual Education. He was also responsible for the oversight of instructional materials being produced in the Audio-Visual Center.

The Center's technological and manpower capacities were increasing, which warranted an expansion of the curriculum. During the 1965-66 academic year, twelve new graduate courses were written as part of a new Audiovisual Media Specialist program.

Lee at UW-La Crosse, 1966

These courses offered an impressive span of content, acquainting students with the design, administrative, and curricular considerations of audio-visual education as reprinted from the graduate catalog:

AV 502: Still Photography
AV 521: Preparation of Projected Materials
AV 633: Audiovisual Administration
AV 699: Advanced Instructional Technology
AV 701: Curriculum and Audiovisual Utilization
AV 711: Communications Media Design
AV 721: Advanced Photographic Principles
AV 723: Cinematography
AV 731: Radio and Television Systems
AV 741: Programmed Instruction
AV 761: Research and Seminar in Audiovisual Media
AV 795: Independent Study

Interestingly, graduate students were not required to take an audio-visual education course as part of the "Educational Foundations" core, though they were able to enroll in any of the new AV courses as electives. Lee contributed to the development of this new program, and is believed to have developed and pilot-taught the "Programmed Instruction" course.

Surely, the development of such a comprehensive program would bring positive recognition to the department and the institution. In March of 1966, Lee and colleagues Vigio Rasmusen, G. Lester Steinhoff, and Clair Rood were invited to speak at the Wisconsin Department of Audiovisual Instruction's annual meeting, where they spoke about LCU's program and other state university audio-visual programs. This organization, which is now known as the *Wisconsin Educational Media & Technology Association**, was organized after World War II as a means of helping teachers integrate "visual education" methods into their classrooms.

Viggio Rasmusen (left) and G. Lester Steinhoff (right)

Lee was also invited to speak at St. Paul's Lutheran Church of La Crosse, which has since closed. After contacting the La Crosse Library, it appears that the church's meeting minutes did not survive.

While Lee's teaching focus remained largely focused on technology, his interest in languages and linguistics continued and he wanted to make scholarly contributions in this area as well.

---

* To learn more about the Wisconsin Educational Media and Technology Association, go to www.wemta.org/about/history-1948-1958.cfm

Part of Lee's dissertation was a programmed text for teaching the English language. Programmed learning was a hot topic within instructional design, in both the United States and Canada. The Programmed Learning Limited, a Toronto-based company, published educational materials that followed the paradigm that Lee's doctoral research emphasized, which included a highly-structured, step-by-step approach to language attainment.

Several drafts of Lee's curriculum vitae list his publishing a two-part text in English structure, however, no additional records can verify this. The process of publishing this text began in 1964, but even fourteen years later, did not seem to have ever come to fruition. Perhaps Lee's other responsibilities did not afford him the time to complete such a large project.

Lee's career was quickly taking shape, and by the time he finished his year at La Crosse, he had spent ten years in the United States. Following suit of many immigrants, in early 1966, Lee decided to legally change his name from Hang Tao Lee to Hamilton H.T. Lee. This new name would allow him to fit in better among Americans.

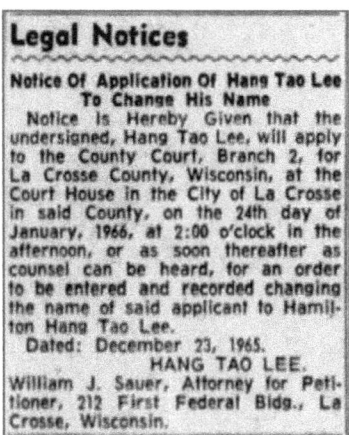

Unfortunately, Lee did not get to see the new graduate program come to full fruition. He resigned from the faculty at the end of the spring 1966 semester. According to an August 14, 1966 article in the *La Crosse Tribune*, Lee's replacement, Donald L. Nicholas, was a graduate of Indiana University. Once again, Lee's motives for resigning after only one year are unknown.

The original Stroud Hall at East Stroudsburg State College, 1967.

East Stroudsburg

Nestled in the Pocono Mountains of eastern Pennsylvania sat East Stroudsburg State College, a four-year institution with a large complement of teacher education programs. Historically, the college began as a normal school for prospective teachers, and even as the institution grew, it continued to emphasize teacher training for those pursuing both elementary-level and secondary-level teacher certification.

In both curricula, undergraduate students were required to complete a two-credit course in audio-visual education, which was the only course of its kind offered at East Stroudsburg. In the 1960s, this course was primarily taught by two instructors.

The first, William Sculley, was a graduate of Seton Hall University who, in addition to teaching, had gained practical experience in media production through work in photography, blueprint making, and motion picture projection.

The second, Earl Slutter, was an alumnus of Bucknell University and had taught as well as served as an administrator in secondary education for nearly twenty years prior to entering higher education. Slutter aspired to return to administrative service, and in 1966, was appointed the Dean of Student Personnel at East Stroudsburg.

Earl Slutter (left) and William Sculley (right), 1965.

This created a vacancy in the Education department faculty. An individual would need to be hired who was qualified to provide audio-visual instruction to education majors.

In May of 1966, Hamilton Lee was offered a position on the ESSC faculty at the rank of full professor. Upon resigning from the University of Wisconsin faculty, Lee and his family moved to East Stroudsburg and Lee's tenure began that fall.

On ESSC Staff

Dr. Hamilton H. T. Lee has been appointed to the staff of East Stroudsburg State College by Dr. LeRoy J. Koehler, College president and the board of trustees. As a professor of audio-visual education, Dr. Lee will be a member of the education department.

Notice of Lee's hiring in The Morning Call *newspaper, July 31, 1966.*

```
                                629 Main Street
                                La Crosse,Wisconsin
                                June 14, 1966

        Dr. LeRoy J. Koehler
        President
        East Stroudsburg State College
        East Stroudsburg, Pennsylvania

        Dear Dr. Koehler:

        I have received your letter of May 16, 1966 regarding
        the approval of my appointment as a professor at the
        College, effective in September, this year.

        May I express my thanks and appreciation for your
        appointing me on your faculty.

        I have requested Wayne State University for my graduate
        transcript to be sent to you.  As for my undergraduate
        transcript, I have written to the Ministry of Education
        of the Republic of China.

        It will be my great pleasure to join your faculty and
        I will be happy to pay you my first visit as soon as
        I am in East Stroudsburg.   Have a very pleasant summer.



                            Very truly yours,
                               Hamilton H.T.Lee
```

A letter written by Lee to Dr. LeRoy Koehler, then-president of East Stroudsburg State College, in response to his being hired.

Lee was one of twenty-five new faculty hires that fall semester; six of which were hired into the Education department. Lee's responsibilities included teaching seven sections of the undergraduate Audio-Visual Education course each fall and spring semester. In addition to his teaching responsibilities, Lee served as an academic advisor to both undergraduate and graduate students studying elementary and secondary education. Lee also served on the committees for East Stroudsburg's 1968 accreditation review by the National Council for Accreditation of Teacher Education (NCATE).

Having lived and taught in two countries provided Lee with a cross-cultural sensitivity that was evident in his scholarly pursuits. His earliest-recorded research project was a study of audio-visual communication in northern European countries.

At the time of Lee's arrival at East Stroudsburg, the only coursework in audio-visual education was offered to undergraduates. The college's graduate-level programs were growing, and Lee felt that it would be important to provide graduate students majoring in education with coursework in this area, too. "The graduate courses," Lee recalled many years later in a personal letter to me, "was advanced indeed in terms of utilizing the very up-to-date instructional materials of many types." In quick succession, Lee developed a series of three graduate courses for the education department, with the first, "Multi-Sensory Techniques," launching in the summer of 1967. The course description read as follows:

> Advanced Application. Theory and application of recording and reproducing devices for instruction situations. Attention will be given to the curriculum materials development and to specific classroom applications (1974, p. 68).

Lee continued to teach this course and the other graduate courses during summer sessions over the next eight years.

Lee never forgot about his roots in China, and his background in English and literature continued to bring him personal fulfillment throughout his life. At the close of his first semester at East Stroudsburg, he was approached by the local chapter of the American

Association of University Women (AAUW) where Chinese history was garnering interest among the members. They were curious to learn more about China, and its origins. On December 5, 1966, Lee spoke on "The Where, Why and What of China" for the chapter, providing a broad, multi-disciplinary perspective on the progress of this nation. Lee's talk, which was reviewed favorably in *The Pocono Record*, addressed factual, cultural, philosophical, and literary perspectives on the origins of China.

The positive response to this talk prompted additional speaking engagements over the next two years, both on and off of the East Stroudsburg campus. He spoke to East Stroudsburg's Literary Club about Chinese Opera; he spoke on Chinese Religions as part of the adult education program at Temple Israel of Stroudsburg. Cultural awareness and appreciation were on the rise, and East Stroudsburg was very pleased with Lee's scope of understanding.

Excerpt of an article published in The Stroud Courier, *ESSC's student newspaper, 1960s.*

Lee surely realized that the perspectives on education from Eastern Asia were insightful, but certainly not inclusive. Scholars in Europe also offered helpful insight into the challenges of teaching and learning. In the summer of 1967, Lee was awarded funding to travel to Uppsala University in Sweden, where he attended the Modern

Sweden Seminar. This event, which had been an annual occurrence for nearly two decades, was described in *The American Swedish Monthly* as "designed to give a concentrated introduction to central aspects of Swedish life and culture" (1967, p. 30). Among the discussion topics of this two-week seminar were Swedish education and literature, two topics that Lee would've certainly found appealing.

Upon returning from Sweden, Lee was contacted by the *Pennsylvania Future Teachers of America* organization. The Eastern Regional Convention was to take place at Bangor High School, located less than thirty minutes from the ESSC campus, and on the docket were workshops about foreign countries.

Since Lee had quickly developed a notable reputation in the community for his knowledge of China, he was asked to participate in the conference. The theme, "Education—No Boundaries" seemed very fitting for Lee, whose approach to teaching and scholarship seemed to surpass many boundaries.

From left: Professors Joseph Kernaghan, Phyllis A. Kistler, and Hamilton Lee, 1967.

The first three years of Lee's tenure at East Stroudsburg were very busy but rewarding. He was an active member of the National Society for Programmed Instruction, the National Educational Broadcasters Association, and DAVI, the Department of Audio-Visual Instruction within the National Education Association. His scholarly involvement warranted his biography being included in the 1968 edition of *American Men of Science*, edited by The Jacques Cattell Press of New York, and by this time, he was well-known throughout northeastern Pennsylvania for his knowledge of Chinese history and culture.

Big changes were about to take place at East Stroudsburg. Early into Lee's tenure, the main academic building on campus, Stroud Hall, had been demolished.

Construction of a new academic complex was well underway by 1969, and it was clear from the offset that this new facility would be the vehicle to bring East Stroudsburg up to present-day in terms of audio-visual technologies, an area in which the college as a whole was severely lacking. The plans called for the installation of projectors, wiring in closed-circuit television, and establishment of an educational media center that housed media production facilities. The administration needed someone to manage this massive effort.

In the spring of 1969, Lee's colleague, William Sculley, retired from teaching. His successor was Michael Weaver, a graduate of Temple University. Weaver came to East Stroudsburg with a strong record of accomplishment in educational media production, project direction, and technology integration. The timing of Weaver's hiring was perfect.

The president of the college, Frank D. Sills, created an Educational Communications and Technology Council that was tasked with determining the process of implementing a campus-wide Educational Communications program. Lee was not selected to serve on this council.

After completing his first year on the faculty, Weaver was named director of the college's Educational Media program. Working in concert with the Council, Weaver led the construction and outfitting of a two-story communications center, which housed the first color television studio among any of the Pennsylvania State Colleges. All of this was completed without any input or involvement from Lee.

Hamilton Lee and Michael Weaver, 1970.

East Stroudsburg's nearly-completed Communications Center, 1970.

While all of this was taking place, Lee continued to teach the undergraduate course in audio-visual education.

Lee received a wonderful honor in 1970 when the Simon and Schuster publishing company commissioned him to develop an edited anthology for educators. The comprehensive volume, titled *Readings in Instructional Technology*, comprises twenty-six scholarly articles about Programmed Learning and Instruction, Technological Implications in Education, and Instructional Television. The latter aligned closely with East Stroudsburg's plan for implementing an instructional television program in the new communications center. "The book as a whole," according to Lee, "aims to orient the student of audiovisual education toward the new perspectives and to reinforce his present knowledge of teaching techniques" (1970, n. pag.). In the book's preface, Lee sheds light on the international movement to provide teacher education majors with additional audio-visual training.

> Both in this country and Europe, colleges and universities are continually strengthening their offerings in audiovisual education at both undergraduate and grad- uate levels. At the same time, the content of audiovisual education is being increasingly extended to include the new concepts in learning, and to employ the technological procedures that are so abundantly available in the teaching-learning situation (1970, n. pag.).

Though it was clear that Lee was aware of the major developments taking place in the field, it was also clear that Lee's emphasis was on the theoretical facets of teaching with media, as opposed to the technological competencies that students needed.

Even in the college's plans for the construction of the new Stroud Hall, the audio-visual laboratory was to be placed on the first floor, in conjunction with the psychology department, rather than with both the elementary and professional and secondary education departments on the second floor.

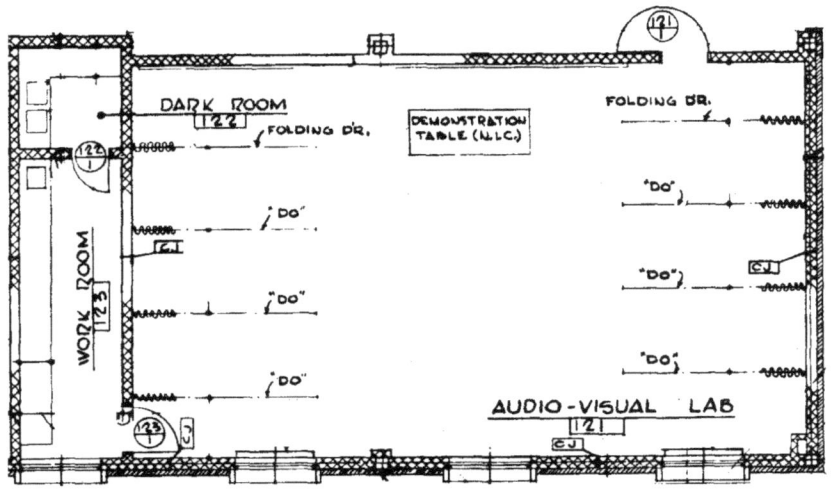

The floor plan for the audio-visual laboratory in Stroud Hall.

A seemingly trivial detail, but rather telling of the college's philosophy at the time, preferring to place audiovisual education with the psychology department. The college seemed interested in studying the sensory effects of new audiovisual technology versus placing the lab with the education faculty where students could develop materials for pedagogical purposes.

In January 1970, the new audio-visual laboratory opened in room 118, Stroud Hall. "That room was equipped with individual learning stations, media production equipment such as photographic cameras and filmmaking equipment," recalled Weaver in an informal collection of memories submitted to the department. "There was also a small dark room in that facility." This was certainly a huge step forward and having a new facility with modern equipment certainly made Lee's job a lot easier, but more changes were on their way.

By the early 1970s, the label "audio-visual" had become outmoded, so Weaver decided to rename the undergraduate course "Educational Communications" to reflect new content. To ensure that each of the multiple sections of the course was receiving the same instruction, as part of the redesign of the course, it was decided to split the course into separate lecture and lab sessions. Three, one-hour lecture sessions of eighty students each would disperse into fifteen lab sections. A special component of the new course was micro-teaching opportunities, or the ability for students to demonstrate their teaching strategies while being videotaped. Overall, the emphasis of the course shifted greatly from the psychology of audio-visuals toward the production of materials themselves.

As 1970 came toward a close, the communication center was quickly nearing completion. A new faculty member, David Campbell[*], was hired with the directive to design and teach new courses in television production. Campbell, who came to East Stroudsburg from Clarion State College in western Pennsylvania, had experience in teaching television and had played a role in the development of Clarion's graduate program in communication.

The final change, at the advice of the Educational Communications council, was to develop a new academic department that was separate from the Department of Professional and Secondary Education. Beginning in the fall of 1971, the Department of Educational Communications and Technology was established, and coursework in television production, filmmaking, photography, and educational media commenced in the new communications center.

Aside from their teaching responsibilities, Lee, Weaver, and Campbell would also be responsible for administering the media production and training services offered by the Communications Center. From an outsider's point of view, being part of these developments seems like a very exciting opportunity for a faculty member.

---

[*] **David Scott Campbell (1941–2015)** taught at East Stroudsburg from 1970 until 2000. See Costa's *David Campbell: Story of a Career* (Masthof Press, 2018) for more information.

The Department of Educational Communications and Technology, 1971–72. From left: David Campbell, Michael Weaver, Hamilton Lee.

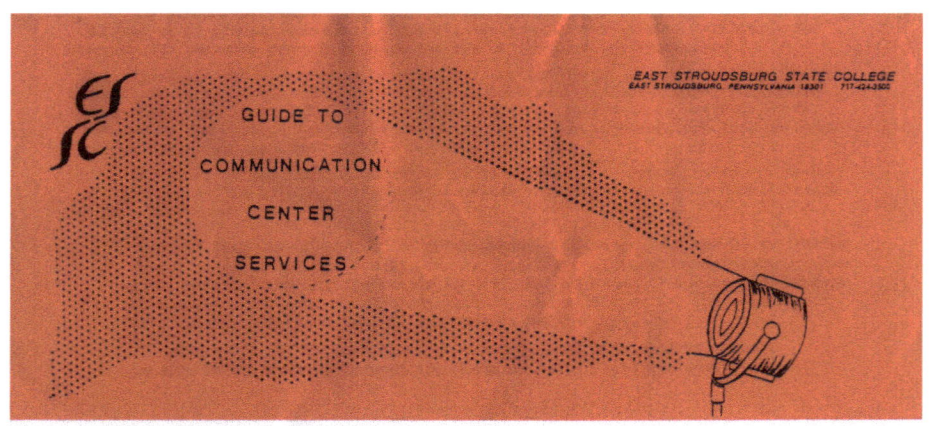

COMMUNICATION CENTER/INSTRUCTIONAL DEVELOPMENT

TECHNICAL CONSULTATION AND REPAIR

AUDIO-VISUAL EQUIPMENT LOAN

AUDITORIUM SCHEDULING
MEDIA MATERIALS PRODUCTION

GENERAL INFORMATION

TELEVISION PRODUCTION/VIDEOTAPE PLAYBACK
NEW EQUIPMENT PURCHASE

A 1970s brochure for the Communication Center's on-campus services.

Reflecting on the origins of the department years later in personal letters, Lee presents a different response to the transition:

> No one asked and no one was asked to be teaching in the lovely established Department of Educational Communications and Technology. All of the three faculty members were, as a matter of course, to be the newly organized unit staff.

Lee's seeming lack of enthusiasm makes sense. Whether because of pedagogical differences or perceived language barriers that some university personnel remembered but would not address on the record, his colleagues largely excluded him from departmental affairs.

Lee was not given an office in the Communications Center and rarely taught courses there. It is alleged that he was never even given a key to the building.

While Weaver and Campbell flourished with new courses and advanced media equipment, Lee was assigned only lab sections of the newly re-designed Educational Communications course, which followed a curriculum that was managed by Campbell, who taught the lecture sections.

Students noticed the disconnect between Lee and the rest of his department. "Dr. Lee never came across to the other building," recalled Michael D'Angelo, a 1975 graduate of East Stroudsburg. "He was the old school A-V guy. He had no interest in the new things." A colleague recalls him as "not in any way cutting edge, was not much of a teacher, and some of the other faculty felt he was kind of a drag on the department." Another colleague, Elzar Camper, recalled in a recorded interview from 2011 the degree of separation:

> He was not as integral a part of the department as I thought he should be. His office was in a different building, his talents seemed to lend themselves towards instructional technology courses. But I often wondered whether, if given a more open situation, he would've been able to make more contributions to the curriculum and the department.

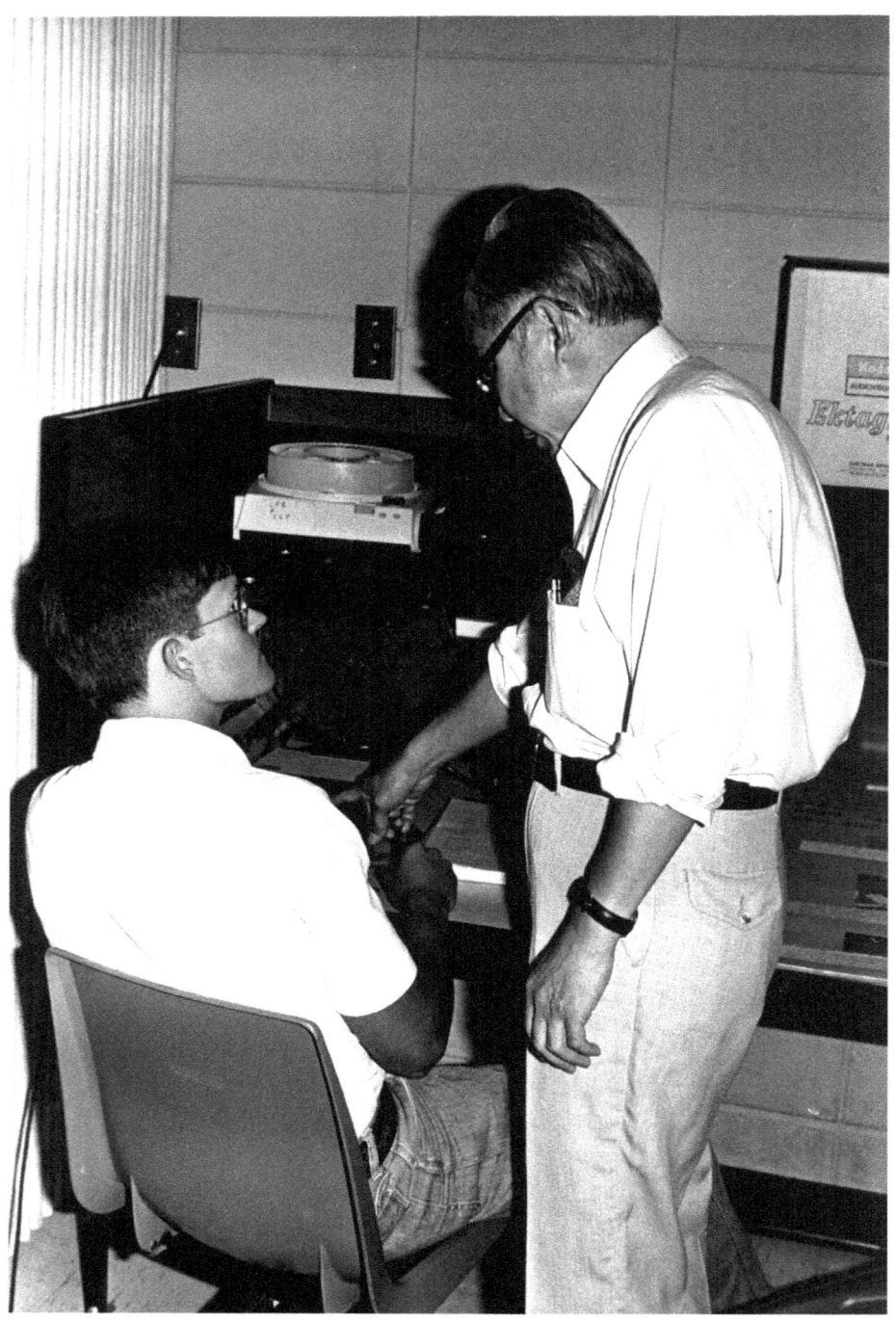

Hamilton Lee teaching Educational Communications lab, late 1970s.

For the remainder of his career, Lee carried a very heavy teaching load: nine sections of "Ed Comm Lab" each semester, where he guided students through the operation of projectors, the production of overhead transparencies, slides, and simple audio recordings.

Teaching graduate courses provided an occasional break for Lee from the redundancy of the undergraduate lab sections, though due to Lee's full schedule, were almost always offered during summer school sessions.

In 1975 and 1976, Lee taught two graduate courses each year. These included "Multi-Sensory Techniques," "Programmed Learning and Systematic Instruction," and "Design and Use of Educational Media in the Learning-Teaching Situation." The following description of the Programmed Learning course was published in the 1974 graduate catalog:

> A survey of recent developments in educational technology; for example, programmed instruction, computer assisted instruction, and other computer applications such as statistical projects research and administrative applications. An effort will be made to give the student as much concrete experience with the methods and equipment discussed as possible (1974, p. 68).

The Design and Use of Educational Media course seemed to function as a survey course for graduate students who had never before received training in media production. As described:

> This course is intended to provide an opportunity of studying advanced educational media. Fundamentals of planning, designing and utilizing educational media and instructional procedures in the classroom and other learning-teaching situations are provided" (1974, p. 68)

Teaching these courses allowed Lee to share his conceptual knowledge of learning and instructional design.

Lee was still very curious about his field, and began to consider opportunities for sabbatical. In early 1974, the University of Michigan offered Lee a visiting professorship in their Department of Communication. Further, Lee wanted to finish the programmed text that he had started nearly ten years prior, and was interested in continuing his own research.

Since the Educational Communications and Technology Department was moving in the direction of offering communication courses in addition to educational media courses, it is highly plausible that Lee was now inspired to conduct research in this area, too.

Eventually, Lee was granted sabbatical leave for the fall, 1976 semester. Among his objectives, he planned to continue his research in programmed learning, finish the programmed text in English language structure that he had started over ten years prior, as well as to conduct research in communication theory. This, atop of an itinerary of educational media seminars, would allow Lee to rejuvenate his practical skills while pursuing research topics that he found personally fulfilling. For a sabbatical that was only one semester in length, Lee set lofty goals for himself, establishing a three-track research agenda.

He investigated education in the pre-revolution United States, the future of higher education in America and how Chinese education had evolved over the past twenty-five years. Lee's research brought him to the College of William and Mary in Williamsburg, Virginia; various institutions in Georgia and North Carolina; and Princeton University, where he was granted a visiting fellowship. Perhaps the most "tangible" accomplishment of Lee's sabbatical was being appointed to the editorial board of *Education Tomorrow*, a publication of the World Future Society.

By 1976, the Educational Communications and Technology Department was investing in its graduate course offerings, creating graduate-level versions of nearly all of its production courses. This also motivated a thorough revamping of the existing graduate courses, all of which were designed and taught by Lee.

In September of 1976, while Lee was on sabbatical, the department updated all three of Lee's graduate courses with no input whatsoever from him. Multisensory Techniques, which was retitled "Selection and Utilization of Instructional Media," was retooled to serve as a survey course of instructional media. Design and Use of Educational Media was retitled "Design *and Production* of Educational Media" "to attract students who wish to increase their knowledge of and proficiency in creating instructional materials for classroom use."

As had been done before, the curricular emphasis was being moved toward the production of media, rather than the study of it. Finally, Programmed Learning and Systematic Instruction was revised to de-emphasize programmed instruction and branch out into other areas of instructional systems design. Subsequent offerings of graduate courses were taught by a new faculty member, Terry Giffel, who was a graduate of the University of Wisconsin-Madison. Like Lee, Giffel came into the department with teaching experience in both secondary and higher education, however, Giffel had just recently completed the doctoral degree and was adeptly familiar with contemporary educational media. Lee was never assigned to teach a graduate course again.

The visiting fellowship at Princeton University opened new scholarly avenues for Lee. Upon returning from his sabbatical leave, one of his first projects was a grant application to fund a manuscript translation through the National Endowment for the Humanities (NEH). Having taught English and being a life-long admirer of the humanities, Lee was interested in bridging his knowledge of literature with his dear appreciation for Chinese culture.

One volume that stuck out in Lee's mind was *The Two Great Poetic Sages of China*, written in 1971 by Tien Jen Wu of the Chinese University in Hong Kong. This book provided a literary analysis and comparison of the works of two poets: Po Li and Fu Tu. "It is a great contribution to Chinese literature studies," said Lee. "The book was well written in a very elegant and simple style (1977, n. pag.)."

Despite the value of this book, it had never been translated into English. Lee planned to embark on this project, which would have involved additional research — readings on the pertinent historical events that took place during both poets' lives. Lee prepared all of the paperwork and provided a sample of the translation efforts, but according to NEH records, the grant was not funded.

It is unclear whether Lee's proposal was rejected by the NEH, or that he never submitted it. The grant proposal may not have been funded, but what was now rekindled was Lee's love of poetry.

Hamilton Lee, circa 1977.

Over the next two years, Lee continued his active involvement with The World Future Society as a contributing editor of *Education Tomorrow*. Lee was published twice in this periodical. His first article, found in the August 1978 edition, reports Teacher's College, Columbia University's then-president Lawrence Cremin's remarks about how doctoral degrees should be required for all educators. A later article, published in February 1979, addresses the need for more coordination between higher education and secondary education concerning foreign language instruction. In the second article, Lee makes the optimistic claim that "A renaissance of foreign language and international studies will vastly aid the improvement of communications and understanding among nations in an increasingly interdependent world community" (1979, p. 3). It is quite plausible that Lee, who had a long-time interest in the study of language, was making a plea to his scholarly peers to prioritize language study at all levels of education.

Lee also remained active in the Association for Educational Communications and Technology (AECT) throughout his tenure. In 1981, AECT invited Lee to serve on the Evaluation Committee for the organization's annual convention. Lee's responsibilities, as described in a press release, were varied and intensive:

> [Lee] was responsible for evaluating several program sessions, one of which was media research and its application to the improvement of media management, and also the reading of research papers. In addition to fulfilling his evaluating responsibilities, Dr. Lee viewed the many exhibits. One of these was the relatively new innovative media-video disc which has a tremendous potential for individualized learning-teaching for all levels of educational institutions.

Despite Lee's long-time fascination with educational media, the 1981 convention was Lee's first and only involvement with the discipline at the national level.

Lee's knowledge of the changes taking place in educational media seemed to be current, though he continued to have a reputation of seeming out-of-touch with current trends. He continued to be shunned by most of his colleagues.

One example, in 1980, came when Lee proposed that computer-aided instruction be included in the Educational Communications course. For reasons unknown, the department stymied the proposal, though graduate-level workshop courses in computers were being developed. Several months later, Lee suggested that the Educational Communications course, which had traditionally been offered as a two-credit course, be changed to a three-credit course to allow for additional instructional time. When his proposal came to a vote, the motion was defeated.

Despite the negative responses he received from the department, Lee continued to remain active as a faculty member. He served on the college-wide Testing and Research Committee and Faculty Research Committee for many years. At the departmental level, he served on promotion, tenure, and evaluation committees for each of his colleagues.

Lee was even supportive of his colleagues' proposal to develop a Bachelor of Science degree in Media Communication and Technology, an effort that had nothing to do with Lee's responsibilities, but still, he supported the proposal. The establishment of this degree program warranted the department to relocate its facilities from the Communications Center. In the ten years since the Communications Center opened, the Educational Communications and Technology department's courses boomed in terms of popularity, advanced-level production courses were developed, and space became a concern.

Following the completion of the new Kemp Library in April of 1980, the previous library space in Rosenkrans Hall sat empty. So, Weaver and Giffel led the proposal for the department to occupy a portion of the former library. Designs for a new departmental suite were drafted that included a secretarial office, equipment check-out room, two classrooms, a computer laboratory, a sound recording suite, a portrait studio, a film editing room, and offices for professors Lee, Campbell, Giffel, Weaver, and Camper. At the heart of this suite was an open lab area that was designed primarily for the Educational Communications Lab sections.

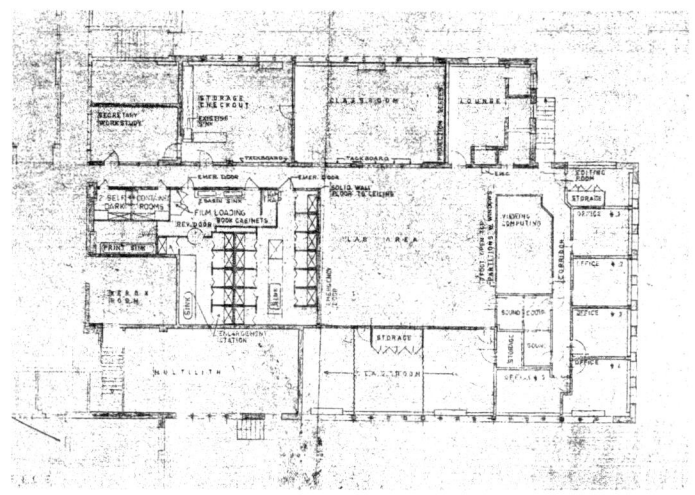

The floorplan for the new departmental facilities.

In the renovation proposal, Weaver described the plans for the new facility as follows:

> Approximately 400 square feet would contain 24 [work spaces that] would support many different courses offered by the department. EDCM 362 Educational Communications [is] currently housed in 118 Stroud Hall. Three hundred fifty square feet will be devoted to instructional materials preparation to be utilized by students in Educational Communications courses, Media Paraprofessional courses, and Communication major courses (1981, n. pag.).

This space, for which the layout was devised by Campbell, would be where Lee would teach all of his classes for the remainder of his career.

The front entrance to Rosenkrans Hall.

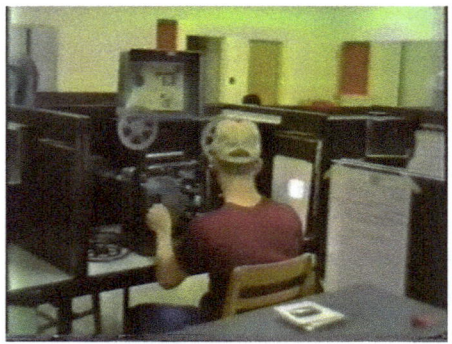

Left: the open lab where Lee taught Educational Communications lab sections.
Right: the computer laboratory, which housed three microcomputers for student use.

In January 1982, the new facility in Rosenkrans Hall was open for occupancy. After almost eleven years of having an office in a different building than the rest of his department, everyone was now in the same hallway. Lee's office was now located in Rosenkrans Room #2.

The new facility warranted changes to the Educational Communications curriculum and lab activities. Happily, Lee was asked to work with Campbell and Giffel to determine the new setup of the course. Work began. Lee's original suggestion to expand the coursework from two to three credits in order to have time for computer instruction was finally viewed favorably. The rationale provided by the department stated the following:

> At the present time East Stroudsburg's curriculum does not have required course content or hands-on experiences with microcomputers for those in the teacher certification program. This course which currently develops competencies in current educational media will develop additional competencies in microcomputer literacy to make East Stroudsburg's education graduates viable candidates in a job market that is quickly demanding such competence (1983, n. pag.).

The proposal also included changing the name of the course from "Educational Communications" to "Educational Communications *and Technology*" to reinforce the technological nature of the course.

A few months before this proposal was finalized, Campbell, who had taught the lecture portion of this course, decided to stop teaching the course. In the spring of 1983, for the first and only time, Lee taught two sections of the large lecture—one at 9:00 a.m., and again at 2:00 p.m.—as well as seven lab sessions. This is believed to be the only time Lee ever taught a large lecture course. Following this, Lee taught one summer section of Educational Communications, a three-week section that met from 8:00 to 11:30 a.m. every day, meeting in the open lab area. This, which had eighteen students enrolled, ended up being the last class he would ever teach.

Lee (second from left) and his colleagues at the 1981 Commencement.

In the latter years of Lee's career, many colleges and universities had established exchange programs for scholars, particularly in the science and technology disciplines, between the United States and China. According to educational scholar Ruth Hayhoe, in the 1970s "there was little serious interest in Chinese education as a model that might have lessons for a wider world. Nor were the transformations to follow China's opening to modernization, the world and the future under Deng Xiaoping or the dramatic changes in cross-strait relations between China and Taiwan, easily envisaged (Chou & Spangler, 2016, p. vii)."

Lee, who had a long-time interest in the history of education in China, thought about the idea of setting up such an exchange program between East Stroudsburg and an institution in China. In 1981, Lee had been contacted by Shanxi University in China with the invitation to serve as a visiting professorship at their institution. Lee requested a sabbatical leave, but for reasons unknown, his request was rejected. Eventually, Lee's request was approved for the fall, 1983 semester.

Lee traveled to China with grandiose plans. He looked forward to conducting seminars for Shanxi's faculty members, enrich his knowledge of Chinese educational history, and enjoy some leisure travel throughout his home country. In addition, Lee had his eyes set on finding an institution that would partner with East Stroudsburg in an academic exchange program.

Unfortunately, none of his ideas came to fruition. It was rumored that Lee, who was sixty-two years old by this point, was suffering from several health ailments and had to return to the United States much earlier than anticipated.

Back at East Stroudsburg, which had recently achieved university status, the faculty and staff fully anticipated Lee to return in the spring semester and continue teaching. However, just before Thanksgiving break, the University received Lee's notice of retirement. In December of 1983, a thirty-five-year career, spanning two continents, nine institutions, and thousands of students, was now finished.

Lee retired from university service on January 6, 1984, and was awarded Professor Emeritus rank later that year. After retiring, he never returned to campus and made very little contact with his colleagues.

His final contribution to the University came in 2006 when Lee and his wife established *The Dr. Hamilton H.T. Lee and Mrs. Jean C. Lee Endowed Scholarship*. The scholarship is awarded to incoming freshmen who have declared communication as their major and can be renewed for up to three years insofar as the student maintains a 2.75 minimum grade point average.

As of this writing, the scholarship continues to be awarded each year to a deserving student.

A Poetic Retirement

In 1987, Hamilton Lee published a poem about reading poetry, which "was written with an intent to convince readers or the audience that poetry is indeed worth reading." One of the many intangible benefits of retirement is that it provides ample opportunity for reflection, and further, translating their reflections into a creative outlet. For Hamilton Lee, that outlet was writing poetry.

Having studied English as an undergraduate and begun his career as an English teacher, it is understandable that Lee's love of literature stayed with him throughout his life. It is also possible that he wrote poetry throughout his life, but after twelve years of searching through library databases and university records, no records could be found to verify this.

The first known appearances of Lee's poetry writing date from 1977, when four of his poems were published in an anthology titled *New Voices in American Poetry*, published by the (now defunct) New York City-based Vantage Press. The four verses are reflective of the human experience and consider such themes as heroism, the human struggle, and our intrinsic relationship with the environment. The following year, Vantage Press published more of his verses in the 1978 edition of the anthology.

Over the next three years, Lee's poetry was included in several anthologies, including *The Honey Creek Anthology of Contemporary Poetry*, *Poetic Treasures–Past and Present*, and the 31st Edition of the *National Poetry Anthology*. All the while, he entered his poetry into contests across the country.

Lee's first recognition for his writing came in 1981 when he received a Certificate of Merit from *The Nashville Newsletter*. Later that year, Rainbow Books, who sponsored *The Edward A. Fallot Poetry Competition*, awarded Lee an honorable mention. Further, Ursus Press bestowed him with a poetry award.

Lee's writing also caught the attention of the editorial staff of *Poetry North Review*. Upon accepting his poem, "Belief," for publication, the editor wrote to Lee, saying "…I found the poem to be very moving and I really liked your style of word utilization (1982)."

According to press releases by East Stroudsburg, Lee's poetry was quickly garnering much acclaim, as it "touched upon various themes ranging from light-hearted or humorous verses to serious poetry," according to a press release by East Stroudsburg State College. All of this acclaim resulted in Lee being elected into the Poetry Society of America (PSA) in the spring of 1982. According to a press release, "the criterion for membership to the PSA is based on the poet's writing and publishing merits (1982)."

In his first five years of publishing poetry, Lee's verses largely focused on human feelings and an appreciation for nature. Upon reaching age sixty, his poetry started to become more reflective on emotions that, perhaps, he had buried in his mind. Just before the end of 1982, Lee wrote a poem titled "Leaving Home Forever," which reflects on his departure for the United States to pursue his graduate degree. During the next two years, verses such as "Mother's Wishes" (1983) and "Mother's Telepathic Word" (1984) speak to Lee's love for his mother and fondness of his childhood home. In addition to Lee's longing for the warmth of his past, it is conceivable that the burden of a full-time teaching load and planning for an ambitious sabbatical leave were weighing on him.

During his final semester of classroom teaching, he published two poems: "Pace of Life," which rather bluntly implies exhaustion, and "Whiling Away," which focuses on the social periods of one's workday with a sense of discontent. By the time Lee retired from East Stroudsburg University, he had received two more poetry awards: an honorable mention in *Peteranodon Magazine*'s poetry contest; and an "excellence" rating by Rainbow Books' second annual *Edward A. Fallot Poetry Competition*.

Now that Lee was free from the nine-to-five grind of full-time employment, he was free to devote all of his energy to writing, as noted by a 1985 press release: "Dr. Lee continues to write poetry which reflects his insights into the matters of daily living. He had had several of his poems published in magazines and anthologies in the past ten years (1985)." Among his publication credits are *Our World's Best Loved Poems*, World of Poetry Press; *American Muse: A Treasury of Lyric Poetry*, Fine Arts Press; and *Words of Praise: A Treasury of Religious and Inspirational Poetry*, American Poetry Association. In addition, many of Lee's poems was published in poetry magazines *Byline* and *Poets at Work* throughout the 1980s and 1990s.

Poetry had become such a huge part of Lee's life. Aside from honing his craft, Lee joined the Poetry Society of America and the Pennsylvania Poetry Society where he was able to engage in discussion with like-minded creatives who relished the poetry genre.

When a publisher works with a writer on a project, a professional bond is formed. For Lee, this happened the most intrinsically with the World of Poetry Press, who bestowed Lee with a Golden Poet Award in 1985, an Award of Merit in 1986, additional Golden Poet Awards in 1987 and 1988, and an Award of Merit Certificate in 1989. Upon notifying Lee of his first award, poetry editor Eddie Lou Cole wrote, "We love you here at World Poetry and this award is our way of honoring you for your outstanding contribution to poetry. Bless you! (1986)." This would be the first of several honors Lee received for his poetry.

Just before retiring, Lee announced his intent to prepare a book of his own poetry. After six years of creative labor, the first of two self-published chapbooks, *Reflection*, was released in 1989. Unfortunately, no copies of this volume could be found. In 1992, Lee's second chapbook, *Revelation*, was released. "The chapbook," as described in a press release, "consists of forty poems in three categories: Insight and

Intuition, Feeling and Emotion, and Light Hearted and Miscellaneous verses." By the time this second chapbook was released, Lee was publishing several poems each year, had won over a dozen awards, and been awarded several biographical listings for his writing.

By 1993, Lee was gaining national and international recognition for his work. It was during that year when he was invited to participate in the Third Annual Society of Poets' Conference and Symposium, held in Washington, D.C. At the symposium, Lee read his poem "Going Back Home," which depicts Lee's first visit to his hometown in more than thirty years. Sadly, his childhood home had been demolished to make way for modern-day buildings, and the whereabouts of several of his friends were unknown. The depth and emotion of his writing earned him the *1993 Editor's Choice Award* from the National Library of Poetry, and in 1994, prompted his receiving the *Poetry of Merit Award* from the International Society of Poets.

At the dawning of the twenty-first century, Lee had published over seventy poems, won nearly fifteen awards, was included in over thirty different biographical indexes, and was actively serving as a board member for an international organization.

Lee was once again interested in assembling a book of his own poetry, as he had certainly amassed many verses since his last chapbook was released nearly ten years prior. It is unclear as to whether or not his family influenced him to pursue this project, or if Lee chose to assemble this book on his own motivation.

He selected eighty-one of his poems, including the first four of his poems that were published in *New Voices in American Poetry* back in 1977. The book, released in 2002, was tenderly and appropriately dedicated as follows:

The book is affectionately dedicated in memory of my respectable and admirable mother, H.Y. Lee (Mrs. P. Y. Lee), whom I loved so dearly and very deeply. But due to some travel hindrance I've never been able to visit with her ever since I left home more than half a century before. For all the years past I've craved for and dreamt of getting back to my hometown and having a mother-son reunion, a dream which won't and can never come true, Nevermore (2002).

The covers of Lee's poetry books.

Similar to his 1992 chapbook, *Revelation*, Lee organized this new book, titled *Inspiration and Perspective,* into four parts: Feeling and Emotion, Insight and Intuition, Nature, and Miscellaneous and Light-Hearted Verses.

Five years later, in 2007, Lee released a Chinese version of the book, titled *Shu Yu Yuen,* which demonstrates his unwavering connection to his home country that he so rarely got to visit later in life. Following the release of the second book, it is believed that Lee stopped writing poetry, as no subsequent publications of Lee's work could be located.

In 2012, I was able to reach a relative of Lee's on the telephone, who would not allow me to speak with him, as he was ill—with no further explanation. On March 4, 2018, Hamilton Lee passed away in San Jose, California, at the age of ninety-six.

I remember being told by my college mentor, "never separate yourself from your research" and to include the story of how you came to learn about something. My undergraduate years of study coincided with some of the most profound changes in communication technology: the advent of the iPhone and Google Drive, countless social media platforms, as well as the FCC's digital television transition, among many others.

It was an opportune time to be studying communication. As I prepared to transfer to East Stroudsburg University, I heard a great deal about how the Media Communication and Technology department, formerly the Educational Communications and Technology department, was upgrading its equipment and curriculum, and it sparked my curiosity in the past.

Has this rate of change been a constant theme in this program? Soon after beginning my coursework in 2010, I developed a fascination with my department's history, an interest that quickly grew from technological advancements to the people who implemented these changes. Upon perusing the University's catalog collection in Kemp Library, I stumbled across Hamilton Lee's name.

In my idle conversations with the senior faculty, Lee's name never came up, or if it did, it was in very minimal quantity. With the help of the University Relations Office, I found a biographical file that contained old press releases about Lee. Much of the records were about Lee's poetry, rather than about his scholarly accomplishments. While helpful, it did not provide me with much insight. Upon learning about Lee's book, *Readings in Instructional Technology*, I remember having to request the assistance of library clerk to find it. Eventually, on a low shelf, we found it.

The amalgamation of my interest in departmental progress was a one-hour documentary that traced forty years of technological and academic history. In putting this video together, I reviewed archival records in the library and alumni center, screened hours of VHS tapes, scanned hundreds of photographic slides, and reviewed the biographical files in the University Relations office. The goal was to showcase the uses of technology over forty years, highlighting major milestones in technological progress.

4-23-10

Dear Mr Costa

Thank you for your letter of April 1, 2010 about your project

In interview I feel it is not so easy to do because of my hearing deficiency problem. So may I suggest that you send me a questionnaire or a list of points that you intend to know. Please consider my idea

Best regards

Sincerely
Hamilton Li

Lee's reply to my letter about the documentary project.

Since Lee was one of the three founding faculty members of the department, I was determined to include him in the project.

The only means I had to reach him was a P.O. Box in Los Altos, California. Throughout 2010 and 2011, we corresponded several times. By this point, Lee was approaching ninety years of age, so his responses were minimal, but very much appreciated. When the project was completed, stupidly, I forgot to send Lee a copy.

Ten years passed quickly by. While packing for a trip to Pittsburgh, I stumbled across a manila folder containing my photocopies of Lee's press releases and other source material I had saved about him. At the time, I had started writing a series of articles for *American National Biography*, and my happening upon the old records could not have happened at a better time.

The managing editor supported my idea to write an article about Lee. My curiosity about Lee was rekindled, but even more, now that I could focus on him as a person, as opposed to him in conjunction with a departmental history. With the help of my colleagues, I was able to track down Lee's poetry publications, once irrelevant to my work, but now invaluable. My English professor at ESU, Dr. Rhonda Ray, helped me with this article and offered much encouragement.

When one is tasked with telling the story of another's life, at least in the opinion of this writer, they must attempt to be accurate and clear. In most situations, the writer is deluged with information and must carefully decide what to leave out or deem "unnecessary." I was not fortunate enough to be in this quandary, as I had very little information to work with. I openly admit that there is a lot that is unknown about Hamilton Lee, and hopefully one day, we can learn more about him.

Putting aside the seemingly linear assemblage of facts about Lee's accomplishments, one conclusion can be presented. Technology did not impress Lee, but rather, he was interested in what it could do for learning. Lee cared about making learning accessible and attainable for students despite the limitations they may face in their schooling environment. Technology was and still is a logical means to circumvent problems such as space and time. Unfortunately for Lee, he found himself in faculty positions that required less of an intellectual approach and more of a practical, skills-based situation. Lee was not a producer of media, but rather, a problem solver who discovered the issues that visual materials could help rectify.

In his doctoral dissertation, Lee articulates a vision for improving education in Taiwan through the use of structured learning experiences accompanied by television segments. One could argue that Lee's ideas were ahead of their time, as today's schools make generous use of video segments and self-paced instructional materials. Lee's proposed "routine of daily learning" for students included self-study using media (1964), which, thanks to the advent of the World Wide Web, eventually became a major catalyst for educational change. "Students will spend much of their time working at home on a major part of their instructional program" (1964, p. 139). In implementing this system, a teacher could spend less time presenting information and instead devote more time to individual conferencing for students. Recent milestones in education, such as the development of "The Flipped Classroom Model," distance learning pedagogies, and the myriad of virtual learning formats brought about by the Coronavirus Pandemic, echo many of the insights that Lee presented in his research.

Certainly, Lee was not alone in his hypotheses, however, we can be proud of him for having his finger on the right pulse. We can only wonder what he would have thought of the instructional technologies available in today's classrooms, or more importantly, how they are used. Evidenced by his later publications not pertaining to technology but instead to language instruction and the writing of poetry, Lee's heart was not in testing every technological development and measuring its effects, but instead, in learning and developing an appreciation for one another. "The social function of education," said Lee, "is transmitting the assets of human civilizations of the past to the next generation. This function should be fully and effectively carried out through all available means" (1964, p. 1).

Also of particular note: "Although the number of media for communication have increased greatly, the personal influence of the communicator (in the learning situation, the teacher) still remains unchanged" (1964, p. 10). Technology is not as important as the content being taught, and the people in the classroom.

A collage of photographs depicting students producing media through the decades. Hamilton Lee's teaching career spanned many years…and many media.

Appendices

Resume

1. Academic Background:

    B.A. National Peiping Teachers University, 1948
          (General Studies and Education)

    M.A. University of Minnesota, 1958
          (Educational Administration, curriculum &
          Instruction)

    Ed.D. Wayne State University, 1964
          (Instructional Technology)

    Post-Doctoral Study, Wayne State University, 1964
          (Psychology of Programmed Learning and
          Communication)

2. Educational Experiences:

    Professor, East Stroudsburg University, 1966-1984
          (Graduate and undergraduate courses in
          educational communications)

    Associate Professor, University of Wisconsin,
          La Crosse, Wisconsin, 1965-66 (Graduate and
          undergraduate courses in audiovisual education)

    Assistant Professor, Moorhead State University,
          Moorhead, Minnesota, 1964-65 (Graduate and
          undergraduate courses in audiovisual education)

    Visiting Professor & Director of language laboratory,
          Seton Hall University, summer 1964
          (Chinese literature)

    Research Associate, Wayne State University, 1958-64
          (Center for Instructional Technology)

    Kangshan High School, Taiwan, 1949-1956
          (English)

    Yuanli High School, Hsin Chu, Taiwan, 1948-1949
          (English)

Courses Taught:
    Audio-Visual Education (ESSC)
    Educational Communications (ESSC)
    Audiovisual Education (UWLC)
    Graphics Lab-Elementary Education Majors (UWLC)
    Production of Audio-Visual Materials (UWLC)

Courses Developed (all at ESSC):
    Multi-Sensory Techniques
    Programmed Learning and Systematic Instruction
    Design and Use of Educational Media in the
      Learning-Teaching Situation

3.   Professional Activities:

Visiting Scholar, Harvard University, 1965 and 1966
    (Studied social relations)

Contributing Editor of *Education Tomorrow* (of World
    Future Society), 1975, 76

Visiting Fellow, Princeton University, 1976-78

Visiting Professor, Shanxi University,
    Taiyuan, China, 1983

Academic Awards:
    Teachers' Advancement Fellowship (Taiwan), 1949
    Scholarship (University of Minnesota), 1957
    Fellowship (Learning Resources Corp.
      of East Lansing, Mich.), 1963 and 1964
    Professor Emeritus (From East Stroudsburg
      University), 1984

4.   Non-Teaching Activities:

Moorhead State University
    Advised juniors and seniors in elementary and
    secondary education
    Served on Council on Admissions
    Served on Records and Research Committee
    Conducted teachers' in-service workshops

University of Wisconsin
    Developed graduate courses in educational media
    and methods
    Supervised production of instructional material

East Stroudsburg University
      Advisor to elementary and secondary
       education majors
      Developed three graduate courses in ed. media
      Served on the NCATE (1968) Facilities Committee
      Served on Testing and Research Committee
      Served on the Ad Hoc Committee on Student
       Representation to the Faculty Senate
      Served on the Faculty Promotion Committee
      Served on all EDCM departmental committees
      Lectured about "Ancient Chinese Opera" for the
       Literary Club.
      Established the *Dr. Hamilton H.T. Lee and Mrs.*
      Jean C. Lee Endowed Scholarship, 2006

Other
      Attended a series of seminars in programmed
       instruction, Resources Development Corp.,
       East Lansing, Michigan, 1963 and 1964.
      Presented at the Annual Spring Meeting of the
       Wisconsin Department of Audiovisual Instruc
       tion, Schofield, 1966
      Spoke at schools and churches in Minnesota,
       Wisconsin, and Pennsylvania
      Presented "The Where, Why and What of China,"
       AAUW of Stroudsburg, 1966
      Presented "Chinese Religions" at Temple Israel
       Shabbat, Stroudsburg, 1967
      Served as a consultant in a workshop about
       foreign countries at the Eastern Regional
       Convention of the Pennsylvania Future
       Teachers of America, 1967
      Participated in "Modern Sweden Seminar" at the
       University of Uppsala, Sweden, summer 1967
      Served on the National Convention Evaluation
       Committee of the Association for Educational
       Communications and Technology, 1981
      Read, by invitation, an original poem titled
       "Going Back Home" at the Third International
       Society of Poets' Conference and Symposium,
       Washington, D.C., 1993

5. Professional Society Memberships:

    Association for Educational Comm. and Technology
    American Association for Advancement of Science
    American Oriental Society
    Phi Delta Kappa (Charter Member)
    Association for Supervision & Curriculum Development
    American Association of University Professors
    National Association of Educational Broadcasters
    National Education Association-DAVI
    National Education Society of China
    National Society for Performance and Instruction
    Pennsylvania Poetry Society
    Poetry Society of America
    The Society of Programmed Learning

6. Other Organization Memebrships:

    International Biographical Centre
    World Future Society
    American Oriental Society
    American Swedish Institute
    Monroe County Museum Association (Pennsylvania)

7. Travel Experiences:

    Scandinavian Countries, Italy, Switzerland,
    North Africa area

8. Publications:

    Lee, H. T. (1964). "Design and Development of
        Materials for Secondary English Teaching in
        Taiwan with Future Technological Development
        in Instructional Procedures." Ann Arbor, MI:
        University Microfilms. [Ed.D. Dissertation]

    Lee, H. H. T. (Ed.) (1970). *Readings in Instructional
        Technology*. NY: Simon and Schuster.

    Lee, H. H. T. (1978, Aug.). "Columbia official urges
        required Ph.D. for all educatiors." *Education
        Tomorrow, III*(4), p. 3.

    Lee, H. H. T. (1979, Feb.). "A future for foreign
        languages and international studies." *Education
        Tomorrow, IV*(1), p. 3.

Lee, H. H. T. (1989). *Reflection*.
   [Self-published chapbook]

Lee, H. H. T. (1992). *Revelation*.
   [Self-published chapbook]

Lee, H. H. T. (2002). *Inspiration and Perspective*.
   Owings Mills, MD: Watermark Press.

Lee, H. H. T. (2007). *Shen yu xing*. Owings Mills, MD:
   Watermark Press.

Poetry in the following publications:

A Celebration of Poets, 1999
America at the Millennium, the best Poems and Poetry
  of the 20th Century, 2000
American Muse: A Treasury of Lyric Poetry, 1985
American Poetry Anthology, 1983
Best Poems of the '90s, 1997
Byline, 1981-1983
Contemporary Poets of America and Britain, 1994
Honey Creek Anthology of Contemporary Poetry, 1978
Insights and Innovations, 1983
Lyrical Fiest—A Poetry Festival in Print, 1985
Lyrical Treasures—Classic and Modern, 1983
Nashville Literary Newsletter, 1981 and 1989
National Library of Poetry, 1997 and 1995
National Poetry Anthology, 1980
New Voices in American Poetry, 1977 and 1978
Our Twenty Century's Greatest Poetry, 1982
Our World's Best Loved Poems, 1985
Pen Etched Memories, 1994
Poetry of Love, 1983
Poetry North Review, 1982
Poetry Today, 1985
Poetic Treasures—Past and Present, 1980
Poets at Work, 1986-2000
Sound of Poetry, 1998
Today's Great Poems, 1983
Treasured Poems of America, 1991
Trouvere's Annual Unknown Poem
  and Short Story Book, 1983
Verdand Lsuds of Spring, 1998
We Are the Poets, 1988

9.   Poetry Awards:

Certificate of Merit, Nashville Newsletter, 1981
Rainbook's' Honorable Mention on Edward A. Fallot
  Poetry Competition, 1981, Moore Haven, Florida.
Ursus Press' Honorable Mention on 1982 Anthology
  of New Poetry, Chicago.
Honorable Mention, Peteranodon Magazine's Poetry
  Contest, 1983
Golden Poetry Award, World of Poetry, 1985
Award of Merit, World of Poetry Contest, 1986
Ursus Press Poetry Contest Winner, 1986
Golden Poetry Award, World of Poetry, 1987
Golden Poetry Award, World of Poetry, 1988
Hon. Mention, Be a Big Winner Poetry Contest, 1989
Hon. Mention, Eddie-Lou Cole Poetry Contest, 1992
Editors Choice Award, Nat'l Library of Poetry, 1993
Poet of Merit Award, Int'l Society of Poets, 1994
Editors Choice Award, Nat'l Library of Poetry, 1998

10.   Biographical Listings:

American Men of Science, 1968
American Men and Women of Science, 1973
Dictionary of International Biography
International Scholars Dictionary, 1973
Leaders in Education, 1974
Int'l Authors and Writers Who's Who, 1998, 1995
Int'l Scholars Dictionary (Strasburg, France)
Int'l Who's Who in Education
Int'l Who's Who in Poetry, 1999
Int'l Who's Who of Intellectuals, Vol. I and II
Int'l Who's Who of Writers, 1991
Poet's Encyclopedia, 1999, 1997
Who's Who: Poets, Writers, Editors & Publishers, 1985
Who's Who Hall of Fame, 1999
Who's Who in America, 2000, 1999, 1998
Who's Who in American Education, 1995, 1994, 1992
Who's Who in Poetry, 1999
Who's Who in the East, 1997, 1996, 1990, 1989, 1985, 1983
Who's Who in the West, 1995
Who's Who in the World, 1997
Who's Who in U.S. Writers, Editors and Poets, 1989, 1986

The above format is based on Lee's curriculum vitae, dated January, 1982.
The content was expanded by the author to include as much detail as possible.

Academic Lineage of Hamilton H.T. Lee

Lee's dissertation was jointly-chaired by professors Joseph E. Hill and Robert W. Kilbourn. Kilbourn, however, passed away before finishing his doctoral degree at Ohio State University. Thus, this lineage will continue with Hill.

Hamilton H.T. Lee (1921–2018)
Ed.D., Wayne State University, 1964
Dissertation Title: *Design and Development of Programmed Materials for Secondary English Teaching in Taiwan with Implications for Future Technological Development in Instructional Procedures.*

Joseph E. Hill (1919–1978)
Ed.D., Wayne State University, 1957
Dissertation Title: *The Development and Application of a Method for Evaluating Defined Phases of Student Activity Programs in Institutions of Higher Education.*

Joseph Wilmer Menge (1905–1987)
Ph.D., University of Michigan, 1949
Dissertation Title: *An Experimental Study of Sampling Procedures for the Determination of Achievement Test Norms in a City School System.*

Clifford Woody (1884–1948)
Ph.D., Columbia University, 1916
Dissertation Title: *Measurements of Some Achievements in Arithmetic.*

George Drayton Strayer (1876–1962)
Ph.D., Columbia University, 1905
Dissertation Title: *City School Expenditures, The Variability and Interrelation of the Principal Items.*

Edward L. Thorndike (1874–1949)
Ed.D., Columbia University, 1898
Dissertation Title: *Animal Intelligence, An Experimental Study of the Associative Processes in Animals.*

James McKeen Cattell (1860–1944)
Ph.D., University of Leipzig, 1886
Dissertation Title: *An Essay on Psychometry, or the Time Taken Up by Simple Mental Processes.*

Wilhelm Maximilian Wundt (1832–1920)
M.D., University of Heidelberg
Dissertation Title: *Studies on the Behavior of the Nerves in Inflamed and Degenerated Organs.*

Karl Ewald Hasse (1810–1902)
M.D., University of Leipzig, 1833
Dissertation Title: *Observations on the Skeleton Astacus fluviatilis and Sea Lions.*

Syllabus

EDCM 522   Design and Use of Educational Media in
            the Learning-Teaching Situation (3:3:0)

This course is intended to provide an opportunity of
studying advanced educational media. Fundamentals
of planning, designing and utilizing educational
media and instructional procedures in the classroom
and other learning-teaching situations are provided.

Sequence of topics or units:

    I.   Analysis of the following conditions:

        The Learner
        The Instructional Situation(s)
        The Subject matter

   II.   Planning the procedures of teaching

  III.   Selecting appropriate instructional media
        and materials.

   IV.   Utilizing certain audiovisual equipment and
        materials

    V.   Preparing simple instructional materials

   VI.   Implementing multi-faceted approach to teaching-
        learning process.

  VII.   Perspective development of future instructional
        media programs

 VIII.   Evaluation

A Lee

EAST STROUDSBURG STATE COLLEGE   BEHAVIORAL COMPETENCY STUDY

Design Institution and Use of Media   Area of Certification

Identify and list the behavioral competencies needed for effective performance in the specific area	Briefly refer to the activities, experiences and courses designed to develop each competency	Means of evaluation to determine degree of attainment of each competency

To select adequate instructional materials and media for learning and teaching.
 	
  To write behavioral objectives
 	
  To define the topic of teaching.
 	
  To choose both printed and non-printed learning-teaching materials.
	Classroom discussions
	
	Instructor's presentations
	
	Reading assignments.
	
	Presentations of related audio-visual instructional materials.
		Systematic observations
		
		Tests
		
		Reports on evaluation of audio-visual materials.

To use efficiently and effectively the carefully selected essential instructional media for learning-teaching.
 	
  To operate properly A-V equipment.
 	
  To present audio-visual instructional materials as an integral portion of total learning environment.
	Instructor's demonstrations
	
	Instruction on the fundamentals of audio-visual equipment through a variety of methods.
	
	Students' practices
		Instructor's observations as records of students' achievement
		
		Tests on the operation and use audiovisual instructional equipment.
		
		Survey reports on the newly developed equipment in the audiovisual media field.

Identify and list the behavioral competencies needed for effective performance in the specific area	Briefly refer to the activities, experiences and courses designed to develop each competency	Means of evaluation to determine degree of attainment of each competency
To design and produce both non-projectional and projectional audiovisual instructional materials.	Instructor's presentation on:	Group evaluation in accordance with criteria.
	A. The process of transforming ideas into visual forms	Instructor's evaluation
To originate an idea for a project(with justifiable reason(s) to do so).	B. Techniques and skills.	Test on students's cognitive learning.
To work the specifics such as converting abstract ideas into graphics.	Students' using mediated instructional materials to learn procedures in preparing audiovisual materials.	Reports.
To produce and complete the project.	Students' use instructional manuals as reference sources for their project production.	
	Students reports on their project progress	
	Students' consultation with instructor about the progress of their project.	

77

Institution
Design and Use of Media

Area of Certification

Identify and list the behavioral competencies needed for effective performance in the specific area	Briefly refer to the activities, experiences and courses designed to develop each competency	Means of evaluation to determine degree of attainment of each competency
To establish and possess justifiable and enthusiastic devotion to implementing essential audiovisual instructional materials in a learning-teaching situation. To compare the effects of teaching(conventional vs non-conventional). To analyze and to prove functions of selected media for certain types of learning and teaching. To thoroughly master the characteristics, usabilities and usefulness of media. To have a pragmatic philosophy of instructional media.	Instruction on the affective learning aspects. Discussion on: The significance of audiovisual instructional media as a great contribution in many ways to the total learning environment. Audiovisual instructional media as an indespensible part of school curricula. The necessity of using certain instructional media to attain the specified terminal behaviors. The justification of using audio-visual instructional media. Students' carrying out the following activities: Reading the up-to-date writings on the above-stated topics. Discussing the impact and influence of instructional media on the process of schooling and education.	Questionnaire evaluation Class reports Discussion on selected topic for students' responses to certain concepts and principl of instructional media.

East Stroudsburg State College

Office of Public Information

EAST STROUDSBURG, PA.
PHONE: 421-4080, EXT. 7

To New Faculty Members:

If you wish to have your appointment to the staff of East Stroudsburg State College publicized in the local and other area news media, please complete the following and return to the Public Information Office.

NAME _HAMILTON H. T. LEE_

ADDRESS _80 ELK St. E. Stroudsburg PA_ PHONE _____

If married, wife's first name _CHIN_

Names and ages of children _WEI LEE, 19; CHANG TSU, 15; YING LEE 12; WAN LEE 10_

HOMETOWN ADDRESS _CHOW Han, SHANTUNG CHINA_

EDUCATION _National PEIPING TEACHERS College_ DEGREE _B.A_

University of MINN DEGREE _M.A_

WAYNE State University DEGREE _ED.D_

HARVARD U DEGREE _Post-Doctoral SCHOLAR_

Others attended _HARVARD U. [Post Doctoral Scholar]_

TEACHING EXPERIENCE _8 years high school teaching experiences 2 years College teaching experiences [six years res. in A-V Ed Communication_

Honors or publications _Scholarships, fellowships from Universities and Institutes_

2 units of English Structure is being in the If you wish to have your hometown and/or other news-papers to receive a copy of the news release, please name _process of_ the paper and town. If you do not know the name of the _publishing_ paper, the name of the town or city will suffice in most cases.

Picture enclosed for use with the release. Yes____ No____

LEE, HAMILTON H.T.
Professor of Education
Graduate Faculty and Undergraduate Faculty
Appointed September, 1966

Earned degrees

B.A. degree Nat'l Peiping Teachers Univ., 1948, (major, edu.;
    minor, general studies)
M.A. degree Univ. of Minnesota, 1958, (major, edu. admin.;
    minor, curriculum and instruction)
Ed.D. degree Wayne State Univ., 1964, (major, instructional
    technology; minor, linguistics and psychology)
Post-doctoral Scholar, Harvard Univ., summer, 1965 & summer,
    1966 (social relations)

Educational Experience

Yuanli High School, (Yuanli, Taiwan, China) 1948-49, Chinese
Kangshan High Sch., (Kangshan, Taiwan, China) 1949-56, English
    and History
Wayne State Univ., 1956-64, Research Associate in Audiovisual Edu.
Moorhead State College, (Moorhead, Minn.) 1964-65, Assistant Prof.
    of Audiovisual Education
Seton Hall (South Orange, N.J.) Univ., summer, 1964, visiting
    Prof. & Director of Language Laboratory
Wisconsin State (LaCrosse, Wis.) Univ., 1965-66, Associate Prof.
    of Audiovisual Education
East Stroudsburg State College, 1966-present, Professor, Audio-
    visual Education.

Loads

Fall Semester, 1966
    Ed 362 Audio-visual Education, 7 sections, 18 hours
Spring Semester, 1967
    Ed 362 Audio-visual Education, 7 sections, 18 hours
Summer, 1967
    Ed 508 (Grad-Level) Multi-Sensory Techniques, 1 section,
        3 s.h., 15 hours, pre-session
    Ed 362 Audio-visual Education, main session, 2 sections,
        2 s.h., 3 c.h., 15 hours/per week, 3 weeks
Other Collegiate Assignments, 1966-67 school year
    Advisor, Undergraduate and Graduate students
    Facility Committee

Fall Semester, 1967
    Ed 362 Audio-visual Education, 6 sections, 2 s.h., 3 cl. hr.
    18 hours

Current Professional and Academic Association Memberships

    *NEA-DAVI
    *National Society for Programmed Instruction
    National Educational Broadcasters Association

Publications

    English Structure, Units I and II (in the process of publishing)
    English Structure, Units IV and V (in preparation)
    Special study of Audio-visual Communications of Northearn European
        Countries

Data Sheet   March 29, 1974

1. Appointment date at E.S.S.C.

    September, 1966

2. Semester for sabbatical leave.

    Fall, 1975

3. Dates and years of service at other state institutions.

    None

4. Dates of all previous leaves, sabbatical, or unpaid, at E. S. S. C.
    or other institutions.

    None

5. Reasons for requesting leave.

    A. To visit one or two universities as a Visiting Scholar.
        (The University of Michigan has offered me as a Visiting
        Scholar in the Department of Communication.)

    B. To conduct a research project on communications and
        perception process.

    C. To finish my programmed text on English Structure.

    D. To develop a couple or more courses syllabi in communications
        and education.

                                        Hamilton Lee

82

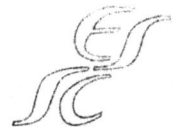

EAST STROUDSBURG STATE COLLEGE
EAST STROUDSBURG, PENNSYLVANIA 18301

July 28, 1976

Dr. Lester Bowers
Dean of Faculty of Education
ESSC
East Stroudsburg, Pa. 18301

Dear Dr. Bowers:

For my sabbatical leave from September to December, 1976
I have formulated a flexible plan. The following are some
projects that I am going to pursue.

    I. To participate in a number of seminars.

        A. The University of Michigan Seminar on Management
            Education.

        B. Inservice/Continuing Education for Teachers, AACTE.

        C. Bell & Howell Seminar and Workshop.

        D. East Kodak Educational Program for Educators.

    II. To continue my research and study in:

        A. Communication theory with emphasis on multi-
            disciplinary approach.

        B. Programmed Learning and its application to business,
            industry and education.

        C. Educational forecast for the future.

    III. To take a couple of educational trips.

Before the beginning of spring semester, 1977 I will submit
to you a report in regard to my sabbatical endeavors.

                            Sincerely yours,

                            Hamilton Lee
                            Professor of Education.

Sabbatical Leave Report
(Fall Semester,'76)
Hamilton.Lee

During my sabbatical leave I was active in a number of scholastic,
educational and refresher pursuits. The following are the details.

I. Research:

I have engaged in a three track research in education with emphases
on instructional media and materials. Namely, they are: the pre-revolution
education of America, the future of American higher education and the
educational development of China in the past 25 years.

A. Through a special arrangement I was given the privilege to use
the unique facilities of the College of William and Mary, Williamsburg,
Virginia, the second oldest college of America, where resources regarding
colonial education are original and incomparable. I have made a preliminary
survey of some of the valuable books and materials in connection with my
research at CWM. For further research on this subject I certainly need
to get there again so as to complete this project.

B. A substantial part of research and study on the future of American
higher education has been done. Eventually I hope that, if everything goes
smoothly, this research will result in a publication of some sort. However,
it will take a considerable period of time to accomplish this goal.

C. For research on education of China from 1949 to the present time
I have been using the Princeton University research libraries. The Princeton University has appointed me as a Visiting Fellow so that I have all
privileges to get access to the resources and materials I need for my
research.

As a matter of truth, the three track research which I have under-
taken will take a period of time to carry on and out. Indeed, I need
some properly arranged time besides my professional duties at ESSC in
order that I can spend some time each week at Princeton for this purpose.

II. Conferences:

While I was at Williamsburg, Virginia I took time to sit in a special
workshop, Humanistic Perspectives. Also, I went to Atlanta as a special
participant in a two-day conference, Southeast 2001, The Next 25 Years.
Themes and topics concerning education for the next 25 years such as
productivity, pententials and adaptive patterns of education were well
covered in the education section of the conference.

III. Educational Trips:

I spent weekends for educational trips and tours in and around
Williamsburg, Virginia. The many historic spots in that area have really

84

enhanced my thoughts with regard to the Bicentennial year. Incidentally,
I centainly think I had my sabbatical at the right time so that I could
have celebrated the Bicentennial by putting myself in the many historic
settings.

IV. Other Activities:

A. I spent about two weeks on the road to visit a number of institutions of higher learning which I had wanted to see for many years.
Duke University and the University of North Carolina were among those
universities I visited. Also, I had a guided tour of Indiana University Audiovisual Center, Bloomington, Indiana and a brief stop at the
Ohio State University early last fall.

B. I am now serving as a Contributing Editor to Education Tomorrow,
an affiliation to the World Future Society.

* * * * * * * * * * * *   * * * * * * * * * * *   Hamilton Lee
                                                          Professor of Ed. Comm
                                                          Jan. 27, 1977

My Sabbatical Leave Plan

As a Visiting Professor at Shanxi University,Taiyuan,
Shanxi, China my primary responsibility will lie in teaching.
It is quite reasonable to predict that I will be asked from
time to time to conduct seminars for the University's junior
faculty.

To continue my research on the Chinese educational evolution and development of the period from 1949 to the present
will be another facet of my sabbatical leave plan. I feel that
I may have an opportunity to have access to the first hand data
(in education) for my research project.

Naturally, I aspire to travel to some of the many historic
and cultural spots of China as many Americans do while they are
over there.

In addition, if our college should like my idea to initiate
an academic exchange program with one or more Chinese institutions of higher learning I would play a role, in cooperation with
others, to take a share in this matter. Incidentally this is
merely my own perspective. Of course, the process of materiali-
zing such an exchange program will take a considerable amount of
time.

Hamilton Lee
December 10, 1982

86

Hamilton Lee
Long Woods Drive
Stroudsburg, PA 18360

11-20-83

Dear Dr. Kemp:

Having reviewed again the whole situation of my retirement I take the opportunity to write you this letter. I would like to be retiring at the end of this semester.

Your approval of my request will be appreciated.

Due to my health condition I came home from China late last September; however, during my short stay at Shanxi University I conducted a few lecture sessions. Besides, I also had opportunities to visit some universities as well as other educational institutions in another province, Shandong.

Thank you.

Sincerely yours,

Hamilton Lee

References

Articles

Modern Sweden Seminar: Initiative and Control. (1967). *The American Swedish Monthly, 61*(3), 30.

Lee, H. H. T. (1979). A future for foreign languages and international studies. *Education Tomorrow, IV*(1), 3.

Lee, H. H. T. (1978). Columbia official urges required Ph.D. for all educators. *Education Tomorrow, III*(4), 3.

Books

Costa, J. T. (2018). *David Campbell: Story of a Career*. Masthof Press.

Hanna, P. R. (1988). Foreword. In J. Kwong, *Cultural Revolutions in China's Schools, May 1966-April 1969* (pp. ix–x). Hoover Institution Press.

Hayhoe, R. (2016). Foreword. In C. P. Chou & J. Spangler, *Chinese Education Models in a Global Age* (p. vii). Springer.

Kwong, J. (1988). *Cultural Revolution in China's Schools, May 1966-April 1969*. Hoover Institution Press.

Lee, H. H. T. (2007). *Shu Yu Yuen*. Watermark Press.

Lee, H. H. T. (2002). *Inspiration and Perspective*. Watermark Press.

Lee, H. H. T. (Ed.). (1970). *Readings in Instructional Technology*. Simon and Schuster.

Lindsay, M. (1977). *Notes on Educational Problems in Communist China, 1941-47*. International Secretariat, Institute of Pacific Relations.

Montaperto, R. N., & Henderson, J. (Eds.). (1979). *China's Schools in Flux: Report by the State Education Leaders Delegation, National Committee on United States-China Relations*. M. E. Sharpe, Inc.

Vantage Press. (1978). *New Voices in American Poetry*. Vantage Press.

Vantage Press. (1977). *New Voices in American Poetry*. Vantage Press.

Dissertation

Lee, H. T. (1964). *Design and Development of Materials for Secondary English Teaching in Taiwan with Future Technological Development in Instructional Procedures* [Ed.D. Dissertation]. Wayne State University.

Documents and Reports

East Stroudsburg State College. (1983, Aug. 19). Academic Year Faculty Workloads for 1982. p. 30. [Computer printout].

East Stroudsburg State College. (1981, Sept. 24). *Ed Communications Center Remodeling* [Blueprint-Detail]. East Stroudsburg, PA.

Campbell, D. S., Giffel, T. C., & Lee, H. H. T. (1983). *EDCM 362 Curriculum Revision Proposal.* East Stroudsburg State College.

East Stroudsburg University. (1983, Oct. 5). Summer Faculty Workloads for 1983. p. 16. [Computer printout].

East Stroudsburg State College. (1975). Faculty Workloads for 1975 [Computer printout].

Lee, H. H. T. (1971). *Syllabus for EDCM 522: Design and Use of Educational Media in the Learning-Teaching Situation.* East Stroudsburg State College.

Lee, H. H. T. (1977). A Translation of *The Two Great Poetic Sages of China* into English. Research Grant Application for the National Endowment for the Humanities (Unfunded).

Rinker Kiefer & Rake Architects. (1966, Feb. 24). *Classroom Building: East Stroudsburg State College: First Floor Plan* [Floorplan-Detail]. Stroudsburg, PA.

Tsu, J. B. (1962). *1962 Summer Language Institute for Elementary & Secondary School Teachers of Chinese.* [Brochure]. South Orange, NJ: Seton Hall University.

Weaver, M. W. (1981, Apr. 17). *Proposal for Utilization of Kemp Building.* East Stroudsburg State College.

Weaver, M. W. (1971, June). *Master Plan for the Educational Communications and Technology Program at East Stroudsburg State College.*

Files

Miscellaneous Correspondence of Dr. Hamilton H.T. Lee, found in various locations at East Stroudsburg University of Pennsylvania.

Meeting Minutes of the Department of Media, Communication and Technology, 1978-1999. East Stroudsburg State College/East Stroudsburg University.

Terry Giffel's Bio File, Office of University Relations, East Stroudsburg University.

Joseph E. Hill's Bio File, Wayne State University Archives.

Hamilton Lee's Bio File, Office of University Relations, East Stroudsburg University.

Donald J. Lloyd's Bio File, Wayne State University Archives.

Neville P. Pearson's Bio File, University of Minnesota Archives.

Theodore D. Rice's Bio File, Wayne State University Archives.

William Sculley's Bio File, Office of University Relations, East Stroudsburg University.

Earl Slutter's Bio File, Office of University Relations, East Stroudsburg University.

Wayne State University College of Education Audio-Visual Consultation Bureau Records (Archival File WSR000206).

Michael Weaver's Bio File, Office of University Relations, East Stroudsburg University.

Institutional Publications

East Stroudsburg State College. (1968). *National Counsel for Accreditation of Teacher Education: Self-Study Report.*

East Stroudsburg State College. (1974). *Graduate Catalog 1974-75.* (p. 68).

East Stroudsburg State College. (Undated, but from the 1970s). *Guide to Communication Center Services* [Brochure].

Moorhead State University. (1964). *Catalog 1964-65.*

University of Minnesota. (1956). *Bulletin, 1956.* Retrieved from University of Minnesota Digital Conservancy: https://conservancy.umn.edu/handle/11299/92266

University of Minnesota. (1957, May 23). *Cap and Gown Day and Convocation Program*, p. 36.

Wayne State University (1958). *University Catalog.* p. 15.

Interviews

Camper, Elzar. (2011, July 12). [Interview by J. Costa].

D'Angelo, Michael. (2017, December 7). [Interview by J. Costa].

Letters

Lee, H. H. T. (2011, April 10). [Letter to J. Costa].

Lee, H. H. T. (2010, June 6). [Letter to J. Costa].

Lee, H. H. T. (2010, April 23). [Letter to J. Costa].

Weaver, M. W. (2012, March 8). [Letter to G. Braman].

Motion Media

Kagel, C. (Director). (1984). "A Promotional Overview: Interactive Video Tour of the Educational Communications and Technology Program." [Still frames from videotape].

Newspaper Articles

Area school hosts teacher convention. (1968, March 29). *The Pocono Record*, p. 3.

Audio-Visual Director Earns PhD Degree. (1965, May 5). *Birmingham Eccentric*.

China talk by Dr. Lee at AAUW. (1966, December 3). *The Pocono Record*, p. 6.

Dr. Lee Acquaints Students With Ancient Chinese Opera. (Date unknown). *The Stroud Courier*.

Education Professor Dies May 19. (1965, June 23). *Inside Wayne*.

Lee to talk to AAUW. (1966, November 28). *The Pocono Record*, p. 3.

Legal Notices. (1965, December 28). *The La Crosse Tribune*, p. 16.

Native of China traces its origins. (1966, December 8). *The Pocono Record*, p. 6.

On ESSC Staff. (1966, July 31). *The Morning Call*, p. 63.

Temple Israel service tonight. (1967, January 20). *The Pocono Record*, p. 11.

Workshop to be held Saturday. (1968, March 29). *The Pocono Record*, p. 11.

Photography (Unpublished)

Braman, G. (1983). *Photo of Rosenkrans Hall at East Stroudsburg University* [Still Photograph].

East Stroudsburg University Foundation. (1981). *Faculty at the 1981 Commencement Ceremony* [Still Photograph].

Photo of Hamilton Lee at East Stroudsburg State College. (1977). [Still Photograph; Source Unknown].

Photo of Hamilton Lee teaching Educational Communications Lab. (circa 1970s). [Still Photograph; Source Unknown].

University of Minnesota. (n.d.). *Photo of Neville Pearson* [Still Photograph]. https://umedia.lib.umn.edu/item/p16022coll175:15269 Courtesy of the University of Minnesota Archives.

University of Minnesota. (n.d.). *Photo of Wesbrook Hall* [Still Photograph]. Courtesy of the University of Minnesota Archives.

University of Wisconsin-La Crosse. (n.d.). *Photo of Viggio Rasmusen and G. Lester Steinhoff.* [Still Photograph]. Courtesy of the Department of Special Collections, Murphy Library, University of Wisconsin-La Crosse.

University of Wisconsin-La Crosse. (n.d.). *Photos of the Audio-Visual Department at the University of Wisconsin-La Crosse.* [Still Photograph]. Courtesy of the Department of Special Collections, Murphy Library, University of Wisconsin-La Crosse.

Wayne State University. (n.d.). *Photo of Dr. Joseph Hill* [Still Photograph]. Courtesy of the Walter P. Reuther Library Archives, Wayne State University.

Wayne State University. (n.d.). *Photo of The Center for Instructional Technology* [Still Photograph]. Courtesy of the Walter P. Reuther Library Archives, Wayne State University.

Wayne State University. (n.d.). *Photo of Students in the A-V Laboratory* [Still Photograph]. Courtesy of the Walter P. Reuther Library Archives, Wayne State University.

Weaver, M. (1970). *Photo of the ESSC Communications Center.* [35mm Slide].

Press Releases

East Stroudsburg University. (1994, Oct. 20). *Faculty in the News.*

East Stroudsburg University. (1993, Sept. 30). *Faculty in the News.*

East Stroudsburg University. (1992, Mar. 19). *Faculty in the News.*

East Stroudsburg University. (1987, Jan. 27). *Poetry Published.*

East Stroudsburg University. (1986, Jan. 28). *Golden Poet Award.*

East Stroudsburg University. (1985, Jan. 22). *Poetry Published.*

East Stroudsburg State College. (1983, Apr. 19). *Poems Published.*

East Stroudsburg State College. (1982, Oct. 22). *ESSC Professor's Poems Published.*

East Stroudsburg State College. (1982, May 7). *Professor Lee wins poetry awards.*

East Stroudsburg State College. (1981, Dec. 18). *Lee Included in International Who's Who.*

East Stroudsburg State College. (1981, Apr. 28). *Lee Participates in AECT Convention.*

East Stroudsburg State College. (1981, Feb. 27). *Lee Publishes Poems.*

Websites

Freshmen/Transfer Scholarships. (n.d.). East Stroudsburg University Foundation. Retrieved May 5, 2024, from https://www.esufoundation.org/_making-a-difference/freshmen-transfer-scholarships

Hamilton Hang Tao Lee Obituary. (2018). Dignity Memorial. https://www.dignitymemorial.com/en-ca/obituaries/san-jose-ca/hamilton-lee-7781672

Weil, A. T. (1963, June 13). Social Relations at Harvard After Seventeen Years: Problems, Successes and a Highly Uncertain Future. *The Harvard Crimson.* https://www.thecrimson.com/article/1963/6/13/social-relations-at-harvard-after-seventeen/

Yearbooks

East Stroudsburg State College. *The Stroud Yearbooks,* 1965–1973.

Moorhead State University. *University Yearbook,* 1965.

University of Wisconsin-La Crosse. *Racquet Yearbook,* 1966.

Proceeds from this book will go to *The Dr. Hamilton H.T. Lee and Mrs. Jean C. Lee Endowed Scholarship,* managed by the East Stroudsburg University Foundation. Established in 2006, this scholarship is awarded to incoming freshmen who have declared communication as their major.

About the Author

Julian Costa is a 2012 graduate of the Media Communication and Technology program at East Stroudsburg University of Pennsylvania. Over the past eleven years, he has taught courses in communication, business, and computer applications at various public and private universities throughout Pennsylvania, New York, and New Jersey. Costa's writing has been published in *American National Biography* and *Et Cetera: A Review of General Semantics*. He is the author of *David Campbell: Story of a Career* (2018) and *A Dream's Destination* (2020), both published by Masthof Press.

www.ingramcontent.com/pod-product-compliance
Lightning Source LLC
Chambersburg PA
CBHW051638120626
46551CB00014B/2128